THE
CHICAGO
AIR
+
WATER SHOW

THE
CHICAGO
AIR
+
WATER SHOW

A HISTORY
OF WINGS ABOVE THE WAVES

GERRY AND JANET SOUTER

Charleston · London

THE
History
PRESS

Published by The History Press
Charleston, SC 29403
www.historypress.net

Cover design by Natasha Momberger

First published 2010

Manufactured in the United States

ISBN 978.1.59629.837.8

Library of Congress Cataloging-in-Publication Data

Souter, Gerry.
The Chicago Air and Water Show : a history of wings above the waves / Gerry and Janet
Souter.
p. cm.
Includes bibliographical references.
ISBN 978-1-59629-837-8
1. Chicago Air & Water Show--History. I. Souter, Janet, 1940- II. Title.
TL721.6.C48S68 2010
629.130074'77311--dc22
2010004905

*To Al Benedict, who created the dream, and Rudy Malnati,
who helped keep the dream alive.*

CONTENTS

ACKNOWLEDGEMENTS

The authors are deeply grateful for the assistance and support from the following individuals and organizations:

Julia Bachrach, Chicago Park District
Bill Cherwin, Lima Lima Flight Team
Chicago History Museum
Chicago Police Department
Bob Coffin, Glenview Naval Air Station Museum
Captain Tom Courtney, Rich Mika and Edward Popelas, Chicago Department of Water Management
Mario DeLuca, Blue Angel Archives, Marine Aviation Museum, Pensacola, FL
Terry Denton, U.S. Navy (ret.) Air Barons Flight Demonstration Team
Major Kirby Ensser, Captain Jason McCree, Major Tony Mulhare, Teddy Rux (Air Show Coordinator), Sergeant Russ Martin, U.S. Air Force Thunderbirds
Gary Jet Center staff
Paul Gavin, Gavinarts, Inc.
Dan Grossman, airships.net
Ed Hamill, Aerosports Marketing Group
Dan Hines, Director of Sponsorship, Mayor's Office of Special Events
Captain Herb Hunter
Petty Officer Chris Laurent, U.S. Navy
Michael Machnik and Gerald Wyatt, Federal Aviation Administration

ACKNOWLEDGEMENTS

Rudy Malnati, Megan McDonald, Mary May and John Trick, Mayor's Office of Special Events

Robert Mark

Gene McNeely, AeroShell Aerobatic Team

Brian Otto, "Hometown Hero," Chicago Fire Department

Bill Reesman, Red Bull MiG

Trudy Schubert, Brian Otto's mom

Sean Tucker, Team Oracle

CHAPTER 1

A NEW CENTURY OF BEGINNINGS

A haze of SPF 10 sunscreen hung above the Chicago beachfront, rising from thousands of glistening bodies clothed in all manner of abbreviated, colorful, tasteful and tasteless summer wear. Lake breezes stirred the rising mirage as an index finger continually thumped a microphone spit cover, "Thump, thump, thump!" From a mile-long phalanx of loudspeakers, a bass voice intoned, "Testing…one, two, three…testing." Ignoring this godlike intrusion, the audience—which would grow in size to over one million hot dog–munching, soda-swilling, baseball-tossing, tubular chair–unfolding, makeshift tent–building, binocular-peering, children-searching souls—prepared to be entertained. Chicagoans had been doing it for fifty years.

Everyone faced the blue-green Lake Michigan with its razor-edge horizon and inviting wavelets lapping at the sandy shore. Most of the horizon could only be glimpsed between spaces in the bobbing wall of power and sail yachts, pleasure craft of all descriptions and the cruising hulls of committee boats, U.S. Coast Guard patrol vessels, Chicago Police boats, Chicago Fire Department rescue boats and Chicago Park District lifeguard boats churning the offshore depths with their outboard motors. The best part was: no one in the audience had paid a dime to be there.

Finally, the high-pitched voice of announcer Herb Hunter—a regular fixture of this event—cut through the hubbub like a saber stroke: "Welcome ladies and gentlemen to the 2009 Chicago Air and Water Show."

Above: Some of the one million spectators at North Avenue Beach with umbrellas and the traditional inflated gorilla on the refreshment stand roof. *Courtesy Janet Souter*.

Left: Even tots use Dad's binoculars to keep track of the airplanes roaring overhead in this 2009 crowd at North Avenue Beach. *Courtesy Janet Souter*.

HERB HUNTER:
SHOW ANNOUNCER

Herb Hunter is as much of an institution at the Air and Water Show as the Air and Water Show itself. Tall, tan and wearing an American flag–themed T-shirt, he takes charge of a room the moment he enters it. On the Thursday prior to the show, he arrived at the Gary Jet Center to meet pilots, talk to the organizers and grant interviews.

Opening a battered attaché case covered with stickers from air shows over the years, he explained, "I keep a notebook

Herb Hunter announcing the 2004 show. *Courtesy Mayor's Office of Special Events.*

here and set it up. One of the things I'll do today is get a room upstairs, a schedule from our scheduler and I'll set up my book. The very first page I have the words to 'The Star Spangled Banner.'" (Oh, yes, Hunter also opens the show singing the national anthem.)

Hunter's book contains every act in the show, along with information he has obtained over the years. He gets information on new acts during the pilot briefings. For him, the real story is the person in the airplane—where the pilot is from, how many flight hours he has, his type of aircraft, etc. Everybody can see what a loop is, or a cloverleaf or giant Cuban 8. But they don't know about the airplane, so he tries to teach. He doesn't work from a script and doesn't start studying for the show until the day before dress rehearsal.

Hunter announces four to six shows a year, using vacation time from his duties as a pilot for United Airlines. Prior to flying for United, he served in the U.S. Air Force and participated in Operation Desert Storm. He has been involved with the Chicago Air and Water Show for thirty-one consecutive shows—first flying in a KC-135 and later doing a ten-minute routine on the Illinois Air National Guard. He got the job as head announcer for the Chicago show in 1988 on a fluke, as he tells it. During the 1986 show, he finished his routine and was ready to turn the mic over to the other announcer, but when he turned around, the announcer was gone.

"Well, folks," Herb said, "I guess you're stuck with me." He went on to talk for ten minutes before the announcer returned. Two years later, he still served as military speaker and national anthem singer but was also asked to emcee the show. He's had

that job ever since. It requires thinking on his feet when there are weather delays, aircraft arriving a minute or two behind schedule or a change in programming. He keeps up a steady patter of aeronautical trivia gleaned from his years of experience while problems are solved in the background.

Chicago holds a special spot in his heart for several reasons: its skyline rising up behind the lake, the millions of people lined along the beaches from Oak Street to Belmont Harbor and the kids.

"It's the reason the show is there," he said. "To have my name linked to this for so many years is very special to me."

What followed was mostly lost in the cheers and revving of boat engines, but everyone caught the gist as they snapped the caps off tasty beverages and settled back to savor the army of city officials, volunteers, military organizations and public safety workers, as well as sponsors and dozens of performers offering their heart-stopping skills.

The Chicago Air and Water Show, presented free to Chicagoans, guests and tourists every year, has become an excitement juggernaut since its creation in 1959. Showcasing the latest in aerial technology and fun on the water, it is the largest presentation of its kind in the world, attended by a cheering audience of three million over a two-day weekend. From the explosive roar of jet fighters to the sky-dancing aerobatics of precision exhibition pilots, the skies over Chicago's beautiful lakeshore are filled with riveting demonstrations of both military and civilian piloting and parachuting above feats of watercraft-handling skills. The Air and Water Show is a unique event of free public entertainment.

It is fitting that this spectacle takes place over the forest of skyscrapers and beach shoreline of Chicago because there is a rich heritage of aviation and aquatic history that runs through the city's past. Chicago's lakefront is not a dump of moldering warehouses and heavy industry; it is a vast open space, a miles-long manicured playground for the people and a host to many events that have left their marks and passed along the spirit of their ingenuity. Pioneers in aviation long ago recognized Chicago's commitment to the infant technology. Back when life moved at the pace of a trotting horse, when Chicagoans were just beginning to trade their buggies and wagons for the horseless carriage, Chicago leaped forward into the new twentieth century.

Only eight years after the Wright brothers unlocked the secrets to powered, controllable flight, the "aeroplane" had matured from a fussy, fragile, kite-

A New Century of Beginnings

Above: Thunderbirds in diamond formation above the Chicago skyline. *Courtesy Gerry Souter*.

Below: The City of Chicago flag flying on the Water Department boat beneath the smoke trails of an aerobatic routine high above Lake Michigan. *Courtesy Gerry Souter*.

A 2009 Heritage Flight showing an F-15 Eagle, a P-51 Mustang, an F-16 Falcon (right) and an F-10 Warthog. *Courtesy Gerry Souter.*

like curiosity into a reliable (relatively) transporter of people (one or two). It carried goods (small packages and mail) overland where there were no roads (logging sixty to eighty miles on a tank of gas) at great speed (thirty to sixty miles per hour).

Chicago's placement at the hub of the Midwest made it an ideal center for aviators. It already had what was becoming one of the largest, most efficient airports—Cicero Flying Field—just within the city boundaries in the suburb of that name, which was incorporated in 1848. In order for a city to provide aviation services, it had to have railroad links. Since most aircraft of the period could only fly in short hops because of fuel capacity and a lack of throttle controls (stop and full speed) to conserve consumption, they mostly traveled in crates over the rails and were reassembled at their destinations. Both the Chicago and Northwestern Railway and the Chicago & Alton Railroad served Cicero.

Reaching way back, the first aerial ascension over Chicago that caused a public fuss and astonishment was on July 4, 1855, when Silas M. Brooks

Three of "Chicago's Finest" inspect a 1911 Bleriot monoplane in Grant Park. *Courtesy Chicago Historical Museum.*

piloted the gas balloon *Eclipse.* Balloonists flocked to Chicago during the nineteenth century, and in 1893, during the World's Columbian Exposition, one of the great crowd pleasers was a tethered flight in the passenger-carrying, hydrogen-filled balloon *Chicago.* That breathtaking experience allowed Chicagoans to see their city from a height of one thousand feet for the considerable fee of two dollars.

Fifteen years later, in February 1908, the Aeronautique Club of Chicago was created and had its first meeting in the Auditorium Hotel. That same year, the city hosted the Chicago International Aerial Balloon Race, witnessed by upward of 150,000 people. But though the balloon ascensions and airship races were spectacular, everyone in aviation knew that heavier-than-air aeroplanes were the future of aerial transport. During 1909, Glenn H. Curtiss, the motorcycle racer and designer, made a series of demonstration flights of his own aircraft at Hawthorne Race Track in Cicero, Illinois. Witnessing these flights were a number of wealthy gentlemen in top hats, including Harold Fowler McCormick. These flights and a subsequent demonstration by Eugene Ely putting the Herring-Curtiss No. 9 biplane

Harold Fowler McCormick (left), at the controls of a 1913 flying boat, was a wealthy flight enthusiast and helped fund and promote the 1911 Chicago International Aviation Meet. Next to him is industrialist F.J. Bersbach. *Courtesy Library of Congress, George Grantham Bain Collection.*

through its paces prompted McCormick—who later founded the Aero Club of Illinois—and airmail pioneer Charles Dickinson to consider creating an event that would showcase the progress of aviation.[1]

Chicago found a true aviation champion in Harold F. McCormick, a member of the family that owed their fortunes to Cyrus McCormick, inventor of the mechanical reaper that revolutionized agriculture. Harold was obsessed with anything related to flight. In April 1911, the table was cleared in a private dining room of Chicago's Blackstone Hotel, and while some of the city's most elite businessmen dipped into the proffered cigar selection and the decanter of port moved from chair to chair by a liveried waiter, the host, Harold McCormick, got down to business. Wealthy in his own right and the son-in-law of John D. Rockefeller, McCormick's weight behind any large project carried with it certain financial guarantees. His guests had the political and financial "clout" to make it happen.

A year earlier, the first international aviation meet held in the United States that brought together the best pilots in the world had occurred at the Dominguez Flying Field just outside Los Angeles, California. The meet lasted from January 10 to 20, drawing 226,000 paying attendees out to the field to watch aeronautical competitions offering $137,000 in total prize money. The competitors flew not only aeroplanes but also dirigibles and hot-air balloons. American aviator and airplane builder Glenn Curtiss flew his own aeroplane and took home $6,500 in prize money by winning two events. He flew fastest with a passenger, blazing along at fifty-five miles an hour, and got his plane off the ground fastest from a standing start in 6.4 seconds, rushing down only ninety-eight feet of runway before lifting off. Everyone in drought-plagued Los Angeles was happy to get the entry fees and gate receipts. To add luster to the event, some Americans set international endurance and altitude records.[2]

McCormick thought that Chicago could do better. Mayor Carter Harrison was busy cleaning up the brothels and gambling saloons in the near–South Side Levee District of the First Ward. Chicago's industry and recreation facilities teemed with success. If Los Angeles could corner the aviation industry on the West Coast, why couldn't the Windy City capture the Midwest business? Nods of approval circled the table. They only needed to decide when and where.

Not letting any grass grow under their feet, the "when" for the big meet was set for the middle of August, and the "where" became the venue that had served for every purpose from Civil War regimental encampments, Grand Army of the Republic reunions and sporting and political rallies to Chautauqua tent revival meetings. Created from landfill produced by the Great Chicago Fire of 1871 and named after the U.S. general who helped defeat the Southern states in the Civil War, Grant Park had become the city's "front yard." Stretching from Randolph Street to Jackson Boulevard, the large open space rolled down to Lake Michigan from a vertical wall of elegant architecture along the fashionable Michigan Avenue. No dusty field in the middle of nowhere, it was like a giant proscenium with only the sky for a roof and all that Chicago had to offer to complete the stage.

They called the event the Chicago 1911 International Aviation Meet, and invitation letters went out to the individual exhibition pilots and aircraft

Professional daredevil Cal Rogers flies his Wright Flyer over yachts moored off Grant Park during the 1911 Aviation Meet. *Courtesy Chicago Historical Museum.*

designers, to the Glenn Curtiss and Wright brothers flight demonstration teams and to Chicago's backyard aeronautic tinkers. They invited overseas aircraft builders—Sopwith, A.V. Roe, Bleriot, Farman and Antoinette. Since the future was with heavier-than-air aeroplanes, no balloonists or airship owners were contacted. Only the hottest and best need apply.

As the huge project began to gain momentum, by the time the first nails were driven into the rows of bleacher seats, the first scandals bubbled to the surface. Aviation pioneer Victor Lougheed (later Lockheed) resigned from the Aero Club on the day the meet opened, claiming graft, mismanagement and corruption at the hands of notorious Chicago politician Bernard Mullaney, hired as general manager of the meet association. As usual, investigations followed.

Aircraft manufacturer rivalries would be acted out above the crowds as designers vied for honors and cash. Both Curtiss and the Wright brothers were locked in a legal tangle, and their future success hung on selling airplanes. There were two other rivals. Calbraith Rogers, a rookie to the game of stunt flying but an accomplished speedster, faced off against Lincoln Beachey, a "veteran" daredevil with a full year's experience, in a one-upmanship game that could kill them both.

AUGUST 12, 1911

A crash of artillery fire echoed off the wall of buildings facing Lake Michigan, signaling the start of the 1911 Chicago International Aviation Meet. Pigeons and seagulls scattered into the sky, a half-million spectators cheered and a single Curtiss biplane rose from the well-trod grass of Grant Park. The frail craft's hometown pilot, teenager Jimmy Ward, sat out in front of his wings and yammering engine, flat cap reversed on his head, goggles over his eyes and the control wheel clenched in his hands. He soared above the racetrack pylons, the judges' platform, the packed grandstands, the Chicago Yacht Club and the steam and sail yachts bobbing at anchor and headed east above the wave-flecked lake. Below him, more than thirty aircraft and their pilots awaited their turn to use the sky.

Aviation was still inventing itself. Roaring through the sky at forty to fifty miles an hour one thousand feet above solid ground seemed terrifying to a population still trading in horses for automobiles. The speed limit in

Jimmy Ward in the seat of his Glenn Curtiss pusher biplane before opening the 1911 Chicago International Aviation Meet. *Courtesy Chicago Historical Museum.*

downtown Chicago was six miles an hour, and traffic cops rode bicycles. From August 12 to 20, Chicagoans and the thousands of visitors who crammed into lakeside hotels got their fill of aerial excitement. There would never be another meet like it in the history of flight.

Young Jimmy Ward was the darling of the press, with his boyish good looks and a grin for the photographers. As a local boy, he had been chosen by the meet's organizers to open the festivities and be the first official pilot flagged into the air by officials. Other local Chicago daredevils who had built their planes in their backyards included St. Croix Johnstone. He had assembled and tested his Moisant monoplane at the Cicero Flying Field and then flew it to Grant Park, landing on the graded dirt runway. When his turn came, he took off in a haze of exhaust and burnt castor oil to flutter out over Lake Michigan, and he misjudged the powerful torque of his rotary engine. He flopped upside down into the deep water and drowned before a Coast Guard rescue boat reached him. The only other fatality during the nine days of mechanical mayhem was William "Billy" Badger, who

A 1911 monoplane's tail protrudes from Lake Michigan as a Coast Guard cutter salvages the wreckage and, hopefully, the pilot during Chicago's first aviation show. *Courtesy Chicago Historical Museum.*

tried to outdo a signature stunt belonging to Lincoln Beachey's repertoire: the "Dive of Death." The stunt involved a steep dive at the ground and a sudden pullout at the last second. Badger got everything right but the pullout. He cratered into the field and was mashed into the wad of junk that had once been his airplane.

Jimmy Ward, to everyone's relief, made it back to the field safely and was met with applause. Later, he was joined by a police escort, which made its way through the crowd of well-wishers to a horse-drawn Black Maria. They popped him inside and clattered back between the tall buildings to the Eleventh Street police headquarters, where, having read about him in the newspapers, Ward's first and second wives served him with papers for bigamy.

The incarceration of darling Jimmy was only a titillating sidebar to the portentous events that took place on Chicago's lakefront over the next nine days. Many of the pilots who watched the boy rise into the air that warm August day did so with professional interest. The most daring and skilled collection of "aeroplane drivers" ever gathered stood in front of their recently constructed hangars or next to their Wright, Curtiss, Bleriot, Moisant, Farman or Antoinette *bolides.*

A New Century of Beginnings

Besides the contingents of foreign fliers, the two largest teams represented the Wright Brothers Flying School, all mounted on the Wright Model B Flyer aircraft, and the Glenn Curtiss "Shop," where Curtiss built the "June Bug" and the "Gold Bug" biplanes in defiance of the Wrights' patent lawsuits.

Among the independent pilots flying a mixed bag of planes—many sponsored by commercial businesses—were the real rock stars. Lincoln Beachey lounged in the exposed cane seat of his machine, relaxing after a hilarious flight down Michigan Avenue between the streetlamps and level with the second-floor windows of the hotels during which he tapped the rooftops of automobiles with the wheels of his custom-built Curtiss. He had to have noticed his rival for the most prize money, the newcomer Calbraith "Cal" Rogers, fresh from learning to pilot the Wright Flyer at Wilbur and Orville's Dayton, Ohio school. Rogers's long and reckless racing pedigree was not lost on Beachey.

Orville Wright, in dark suit and bowler hat, was in Chicago with his team, as was Glenn Curtiss, natty in a straw boater and seersucker jacket. Curtiss looked more prepared for a yachting regatta than an air meet. One of his new "hydoaeroplane" Flying Boats bobbed at its pier ready for a demonstration of water landings and takeoffs, which had roused crowds on Lake Erie. The difference between the team bosses extended to the team members as well. Orville Wright managed his team, while Wilbur hustled sales and spent time in courthouses defending their claims against "patent infringers." The Wrights were small-town bicycle builders whose dogged patience and experimentation had led them to the secrets of piloted and controlled flight. Their success did not change who they were. Early problems with the press and U.S. Army contracts had driven them further into a "them v. us" mindset, which fed their need for isolation and dictatorial control.

The Wright brothers' team members—Phil Parmelee, Arthur Welsh, Clifford Turpin, Howard Gill, Frank Coffyn and Walter Brookins—all received flat salaries for their participation in meets, regardless of their success. Frank Coffyn remembered:

We flew at fairs and aviation meets. The Wright Company gave us a base salary of twenty dollars a week and fifty dollars a day for every day we flew. In those days, I was able to make six or seven thousand dollars a year because they kept me busy and I was able to fly without cracking up. The Wright Company never let us keep any of the prizes we won. The company kept them and we just got our fifty dollars a day. No bonuses, nothing. It

A lone Wright Flyer flies above Municipal Pier (Navy Pier) during the 1911 Aviation Meet—a wondrous sight to Chicagoans of that time. *Courtesy Chicago Historical Museum.*

was a sore point with us, because the Curtiss Company allowed their pilots to keep 50 percent of all the prizes they won. We used to get furious about it, but it didn't do us any good. The Wrights wouldn't let us have it.[3]

No Wright team flying was permitted on Sundays, and all flights were restricted to simple flight patterns demonstrating the reliability of the Wright Flyer models A and B. No acrobatics or trick flying by team members was allowed. Death-defying stunts were left to the independent pilots flying Wright planes who paid the Wrights fees for the privilege and, under legal duress, offered up a portion of their winnings to the brothers. Another strict rule was "No Women Allowed," either as passengers or as pilots.

Glenn Curtiss was the polar opposite to the Wrights. Despite the Wrights' very personal hatred for him, and what they viewed as his thievery of their money and patented invention, his fame and accomplishments grew exponentially. His spirit of experimentation and love of speed and adventure were reflected in his eager and friendly treatment of both clients and associates. His exhibition team members shared in the prize money they won, in addition to their salaries. Despite the Wrights' legal railings and injunctions, Curtiss persisted, and a constant stream of clients wanting airplanes visited his Hammondsport,

New York shop. His perfection of the floatplane resulted in another shop opening in California. He relished his chance to cash in on the success of his airplanes with a worldwide audience.

The 1911 Chicago International Aviation Meet became the perfect venue for a face-off that included the finest pilots and the most famous manufacturers in the world. Two-thirds of the area set aside for the landing and takeoff field was ringed with seats for an audience of thirty thousand. Seating ranged from plank risers to VIP cushioned bleachers, complete with beverage service for a nominal sum. Since much of the show happened in the sky above the city, all of the seats were open to the elements, which fortunately did not interfere with the nine days of thrills and spills. Out-of-towners constituted a large portion of the audience, so cultural high points—such as fine dining, theatre, opera and the beautiful lakeshore parklands—ensured aeroplane enthusiasts and thrill seekers a complete buffet of experiences.

The stage for the event included pylons erected at the north and south extremes of the field, around which planes flew laps like race cars. In the center was the judges' platform, complete with large megaphones through which they shouted results to the grandstands. The powdered chalk shapes of navy ships were laid out in the dirt for "bombing" accuracy contests with chalk-filled sacks dropped from cockpits. The north end of the park was lined with hangars for storing the planes and spare parts. A taxiway led to the takeoff and landing runways. On some days, because of stiff east winds off the lake, getting the planes up and down proved difficult. The planes' light weight and huge wing areas made them frequent victims to wind gusts that could tip them up and over when they stood empty and exposed. Many low-speed collisions and crashes on the ground resulted during this vulnerable time, but not one aerial collision occurred. Officials controlled air traffic and minimized casualties with a combination of star-shell rockets, loud cannon shots, waving flags and shouts of warning through the megaphones to the audience when pieces fell off the planes from overhead.

The first day of competition—following the opening ceremonies with Jimmy Ward swooping up into the sunshine-bright day in his Curtiss biplane—had to be electric with anticipation. Everyone who was anyone in aviation was there. The stunt pilots either swaggered or lounged in practiced insouciance. They, along with race car drivers or motorcycle speed demons, were the superheroes of the period. Glenn Curtiss was already famous as a record-setting motorcycle racer. They stood out in the crowd with eyes creased at the corners from the searing sun and blasting wind, complexions ruddy from exposure to cold at high altitudes and slightly yellowed from the castor oil that lubricated their engines. The raccoon effect around the eyes from the goggles and the hint of gasoline and shellac, or banana oil, which was dabbed on wing patches, permeated their work clothes.

Amid the milling, rubbernecking and well-wishing came the continuing snorts and bursts of engine noise as mechanics fine-tuned their power plants. From the *bratta-bratta* and *rumm-rumm* of churning pistons to the clatter of wood propellers settling into their buzz-saw whirr, parasols blew skyward, along with bowler hats and straw skimmers, and bobbed and bounced across the oil-soaked ground. From the chaos, pockets of sane activity materialized as revving engines pulled and pushed their spruce and ash wood–rigged canvas kites toward the takeoff line.

Crewmen dug in their heels, gripping the planes' tail surfaces, holding fast as the engines, revved to full power, pointed down the empty stretch of graded dirt. With his hand raised, the pilot waited until the vibrations, rattles and machinegun sputter of exhaust seemed right. He dropped his hand, and the ground crew released its hold. If done right, the plane slid forward on its wheels and tail skid. If not, the nose tipped down into the dirt, shattering the propeller and dumping the pilot out of his seat and onto the unyielding ground. If everything worked perfectly, the collection of canvas, spars, piano wire, wicker, tin gas tank and yammering engine rolled on wire-spoke wheels down the runway. With the engine churning and the pilot's hands gripping the wheel, or steering levers, the great wide wings caught the air, and the airfoil created by the rigid canvas caused the weight to lift. Beneath the pilot, the whirr and bounce of wheels diminished. Faces and waving arms flashed past. The end of the runway rushed at him. And then there was only the wind and the engine and the wheels spinning from their own momentum, shedding gobs of mud. Through the cotton stuffed in his ears, the pilot listened to and sensed every beat of the racing motor and singing wires until, inch by inch, he relaxed in his seat and looked over the side of his cockpit at the ground. All the vibrations felt right. It was time to get down to business.

Compared to today's Air and Water Show, where the pilots put their aircraft through seemingly impossible convolutions with incredible precision and consistency, in 1911, completing a successful takeoff without crashing was worth a round of applause. At one time during the nine days of competition and demonstration, the audience, their necks stiff from craning them to follow the action, counted twenty-five aircraft in the sky at the same time. Considering the precise two-way-radio-controlled choreography of today's show, it is amazing that not one single aerial mishap occurred over Grant Park.

But no ground crew would be able to "traffic control" Lincoln Beachey for the stunt he had in mind. His Curtiss biplane was wheeled out with an extra-large fuel tank bolted on. On the last day of the meet, he was going to attempt a new altitude record. At the Los Angeles meet, fellow stunt pilot Arch Hoxey had pegged the height at 11,474 feet.

With the engine cranking at full power, Beachey snarled down the runway and lifted skyward—and kept on going up. Soon, the sound of his motor faded away. The Curtiss aeroplane pushed Lincoln Beachey up toward the clouds, rising into the cool and then cold air as it punched through a thin layer of stratus. He had only added a scarf and gauntlets to his usual suit and tie and taped his pants cuffs close to his ankles. An altitude-measuring barograph was fastened to his wing spar where he could see it. He climbed higher, and the thin air caused him to take shallow breaths. Higher still, the skin around his nose and lips began to turn blue. At the highest point man had ever flown an aeroplane, his Curtiss-designed motor began to miss and cough, and then the propeller clattered to a halt. He had deliberately run out of gas. Silence surrounded him. Amid the buffeting wind and creak of his wood spars, he tipped the nose over and saw the curve in the Lake Michigan shore and the stratus clouds beneath him. In a slow, controlled series of swooping spirals, Beachey glided—or "volplaned," to use the term of the day—down toward Chicago, down from a new world's altitude record of 11,642 feet, down to where he could take a full breath again. All totaled, Beachey left Chicago with $11,667 in prize money.

His rival and rookie stunt pilot Cal Rogers did not leave the Windy City empty-handed. Rogers's Wright Model B Flyer took him aloft until he accumulated enough time—twenty-five hours—to win the endurance prize and a total take of $11,285. He was so flushed with success that he accepted an offer to fly from New York to California beginning in September for the Vin Fiz soda pop company. With the company's logo painted on the aeroplane, he powered into the sky on the East Coast and landed in California forty-nine days later to claim his money. He had crashed so many times that there was virtually nothing left of the Wright Flyer that had taken off in New York. A specially chartered train had accompanied the flight carrying spare parts. Lashed to the side of the Vin Fiz plane was a pair of crutches for Rogers's broken leg.

The Chicago International Aviation Meet gave away more than $80,000 in prize money. Audiences were treated to rare sights as Glenn Curtiss

Pinafores, straw boaters and derbies were audience fashion statements on South Michigan Avenue in 1911. *Courtesy Chicago Historical Museum.*

dispatched one of his "hydroaeroplanes"—the first commercially successful amphibian aircraft— to pull a downed pilot from Lake Michigan, achieving the world's first air-sea rescue. Famed long-distance pilot Harry Atwood dropped into the lakeside party to great applause while making his famous flight from New York to St. Louis. Pilots in the air when he arrived over the city formed an escort for his Wright Flyer down to the Grant Park landing field. The aviation meet turned out to be the largest and the last of its kind. Harold McCormick wrote a check for $75,000 to cover cost overruns, and the show's hangars were dismantled and taken over to Cicero Flying Field to be reassembled and added to the facility's luster.

Sadly, many of the pilots who participated in the meet were dead within two years. Cal Rogers was flying in California when a seagull flew into his propeller. Lincoln Beachey was testing a new monoplane and something broke over San Francisco Bay. He was dragged down with the wreckage and drowned. Not long after the Chicago meet, Orville Wright closed his flying school and disbanded his exhibition team to concentrate on designing aeroplanes. By 1912, the patented Wright wing warping flight control was obsolete. His arch enemy, Glenn Curtiss continued to battle the Wright

Brothers' patent litigation until he was almost broke. America's entry into World War I caused the government to combine all aviation patents into a manufacturer's pool in 1917 and the brothers' stranglehold on aircraft progress in the United States was released. Curtiss went on to eventually merge with the Wright Company in 1929 and the combined companies became Curtiss-Wright, a current aerospace contributor.

There would be other air shows, air races and air meets, but never again would there be anything in the world like the 1911 Chicago International Aviation Meet, where millions of people were eyewitnesses to our dream of aviators soaring with the birds. They set the stage for a grand tradition that has lasted more than fifty years.

CHAPTER 2

AVIATION LEGACY SHINES THROUGH THE GREAT DEPRESSION

The excitement over aviation lived on in Chicago; flight never became commonplace, even after the compressed nine days of thrills offered up by the 1911 International Aviation Meet. In addition to the Cicero Flying Field, small airports opened up around the city: Ashburn Field (the first to have a "control tower") in Maywood Park and the Checkerboard Field across the street. But curiously, one of the busiest airports in the city continued to be in Grant Park, especially after airmail arrived in 1918. World War I surplus De Havilland 4 and JN-4 "Jenny" biplanes routinely sputtered into Grant Park to drop off and pick up mailbags. Watching the planes arrive and take off in Chicago's front yard replaced sitting around the railroad station watching trains come and go. This lakefront mail drop was the birth of commercial airline service in Chicago.

In 1919, Goodyear Tire and Rubber Company constructed a blimp named the *Wingfoot Express*, which was lifted by ninety-five thousand cubic feet of hydrogen, similar to other blimps the company had built for the U.S. Navy. Their construction site was a former balloon hangar in the White City Amusement Park at Sixty-third and South Parkway. Along with a photographer and two passengers, pilot John Boertner and his two mechanics boarded the control car that hung beneath the huge gasbag and took off for Grant Park. Motoring at a stately pace, the blimp was applauded and cheered as it passed across the fortress of concrete buildings that guarded Michigan Avenue and the acres of greensward that led down to Lake Michigan. Bowing to a request from the photographer for a few more pictures from the unique viewpoint, Boertner steered the *Wingfoot Express* out over the lake. At 4:45 p.m., as they returned to the shoreline flying above the downtown Loop at an altitude of twelve hundred feet, the hydrogen gas suddenly burst into flame.

The crowds in Grant Park who had gathered to watch the giant airship glide above their city began seeking cover. Trailing a boiling plume of flame and smoke, the blimp was in obvious distress. Boertner and his two mechanics, seeing that the control cables had been burned away, quickly stepped out of the car wearing parachutes. One other person parachuted, but by that time he was too low to have his chute fully deployed, and he drove into the ground, breaking both legs so severely that he died later in the hospital.

Dripping flaming wreckage, the blimp's envelope collapsed above the Illinois Trust and Savings Bank building. It spilled down onto the roof skylight, crashed through, tore a flaming path down into the depths of the lobby and burned to death ten bank employees who were closing up for the day. The plunging fireball also dragged the remaining two passengers into the cauldron of fire and twisted debris.

The *Wingfoot Express* crash on July 21, 1919, was the worst disaster in aviation history to that time. Chicago officials raged and clamored to bar all flights over the city. Ordinances were drawn. Mayor Cermak proclaimed, "This accident shows we must stop flying over the city sooner or later and we better do it sooner."

Eventually, the panic and outrage subsided, and air traffic over the city remained unregulated. However, the Grant Park Airstrip was closed, and the property was never again used as a landing field.[4] The U.S. Airmail was shifted to Checkerboard Airport at Twelfth Street (Roosevelt Road) and First Avenue. Later, the mail service was shifted again to Maywood Field, where it remained until 1926, when commercial airline travel arrived in Chicago.[5]

In 1933, as the United States entered the darkest time of the Great Depression, Chicago threw a party. The city made use of its vital lakefront to create a Century of Progress Chicago International Exposition. Its purpose was to "attempt to demonstrate to an international audience the nature and significance of scientific discoveries, the methods of achieving them, and the changes which their application has wrought in industry and in living conditions." This high-flown motivation also included celebration of Chicago's centennial year.

The fair occupied many specially constructed buildings and exhibits that often attempted to convey highly technological concepts to the general public.

Aviation Legacy Shines through the Great Depression

The German *Graf Zeppelin* rigid dirigible visited the 1933 Century of Progress fair and circled the lakefront fairgrounds, attempting to *not* display the Nazi swastika painted on its vertical stabilizer fins. *Courtesy Dan Grossman, http://www.airships.net.*

An area of 427 acres—mostly landfill—was created just south of Chicago's downtown from Twelfth Street to Thirty-ninth Street (Pershing Road). Today, McCormick Place and Northerly Island occupy that area. While only scheduled to operate during 1933, its popularity and the need to earn enough to cover its cost extended its stay through October 31, 1934. Over its two-year run, the fair hosted 48,769,227 visitors and demonstrated many of the mechanical and electronic marvels that would become commonplace over the next several decades.[6]

Transportation was one of the major showpiece themes and an attendance favorite. Detroit produced concept automobiles such as Pierce-Arrow's entry, the Silver Arrow ("Suddenly it's 1940!"), and the famous Chicago, Burlington and Quincy Zephyr streamlined train made a record run from Denver, Colorado, to Chicago and arrived dramatically on stage during a performance of the historical tableaux show, *Wings of the Century*. But for sheer drama, the skies above Chicago once more took center stage.

Germany's famous dirigible, *Graf Zeppelin*, arrived above the city. Looming like a shark swimming through air, the 776-foot airship with a 100-foot girth arrived on October 23, 1933, and circled the lakefront fair slowly for two hours, powered by its five Maybach VL-2, 12-cylinder engines, each developing 550 horsepower at a maximum speed of eighty miles per hour. German authorities had predetermined its course above the city since the National Socialist Party had come to power in 1933, and Hitler's ascendancy was a sore point to most German-Americans. Consequently, the LZ-127 zeppelin was only allowed to cruise in a clockwise pattern above downtown Chicago so Chicagoans would only see the tricolor German flag on the starboard side of the dorsal and ventricle fins and not the Nazi swastika painted on the port side. Considering the size of Chicago, that was like trying to hide a basketball under a walnut shell.[7] The *Graf Zeppelin* touched down for twenty-five minutes in Glenview at the Curtiss-Reynolds Airport, where it dropped off mail, and then resumed its stately schedule ahead of an approaching thunderstorm, flaunting its twisted symbol of threat over the financially wounded United States.

Throughout the 1930s, Chicago got down to the business of aviation, taking advantage of the city's geographic location as the Midwest transportation hub. The post–World War I era had left the United States in the dust as far as aviation technology was concerned. With the military downsizing its forces—in particular the Army Air Service—innovative advances in flight lost their major supporter. Obsolete military planes were dumped on the civilian market as war surplus. Many airplane companies went broke, and only a few survived by forming a trust or exclusive consortium. Tried and true designs that guaranteed profits caused stagnation in the United States, while Europe—especially Germany and France—fell back on the potentials and innovations of commercial aviation to move people and goods because their railroads had been virtually bombed out of existence.

As the United States searched for solutions to ease the ravages of the Great Depression, failed banks, plunging property values, the black hole created by Wall Street and double-digit unemployment, cities and towns tried to provide weary citizens with some entertainment relief. While Hollywood cranked out "talking" screwball comedies, musicals, programmer westerns and stories of spiritual triumph, local communities used their resources to raise a laugh or a cheer. Chicago was no different.

In 1934, twenty-two separate park districts were merged into one Chicago Park District under the Park Consolidation Act created by the Illinois legislature. Following on the heels of the successful Century of Progress Worlds Fair, bringing Chicagoans into the parks and down to the lakefront became a major project of the new administration. As the visionary designer of Chicago's lakefront, Daniel Burnham, once said, "Make no small plans," the new Chicago Park District initiated a series of extravaganzas called Carnival of the Lakes.

The Chicago Park District created many clubs, workshops and day camp schools teaching the arts, dance, woodcraft, music and a variety of sports. Kids flocked to the parks to learn tennis, golf, sailing and rowing and how to bead Indian costumes, play baseball and fly model airplanes. The Carnival of the Lakes became a showplace to demonstrate the success of all of these pursuits and brought jobless adults into the mix as well, both as parents and instructors for small but steady salaries. Beginning in 1936, these weeklong free shows played to big crowds. Anxious and proud parents watched Susie in costume as a water nymph in the decorated boat parade. Tommy performed his front layout dive in the pike position for a trophy, and Dad helped string

The WATER PARADE of the CARNIVAL of the LAKES!

An Entertaining Spectacle You'll Long Remember

• ● •

Chicago's greatest aquatic festival. Parade of beautiful and spectacular illuminated water floats and craft. Sensational sham battles, speedboat races and daredevil stunts. Magnificent fireworks display! Night turned into day on beautiful—

Burnham Park Lagoon

A bi-fold brochure for the 1936 Carnival of the Lakes sponsored by the Chicago Park District. *Courtesy Chicago Park District.*

lights on his neighbor's boat while Mom repaired JoAnne's swimsuit strap. Enough professional acts were featured in the lakefront venues to keep the level of entertainment high.

An example of the variety of these seven-day events can be seen in the brochure describing the coming attractions of the First Annual Carnival of the Lakes.

Chicagoans were treated to a sham battle on Northerly Island between naval reserve officers, marines and coast guardsmen employing the landing of troops, gunfire, rockets exploding, flares arching through the sky and "actual battle implements" brought into the fray. And if that was too tame, everyone trooped down to the lake to watch the "King of Crash," Dr. C.C. McWilliams, renowned stunt driver who wowed audiences at the 1933 Century of Progress. The doctor promised to crash a Gar Wood speedboat at fifty miles per hour into and through a floating house. At nine o'clock that evening, the Burnham Park Lagoon was the setting for a decorated boat parade of lighted yachts and towed floats to open the Queen's Coronation, where Miss Mary Dunbar arrived on her "Alice in Wonderland" float with her Court of Honor enthroned in the Lagoon Theatre. With the week's events properly launched, a shift in time brought down full-scale, home-built models of the *Monitor* and *Merrimac* from the Civil War to battle as they did in Hampton Roads. A more peaceable demonstration involved "Chicago's largest fire tug," shooting jets of water from its cannon to extinguish a

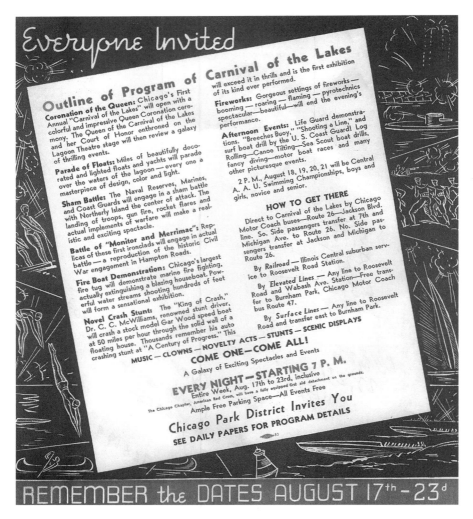

A brochure for the 1936 Carnival of the Lakes, another precursor to the Air and Water Show. *Courtesy Chicago Park District.*

blazing houseboat. Fireworks, lifeboat drills by the Coast Guard, canoe tilting, fancy diving, motorboat races and lifeguard demonstration in the use of the "breeches buoy" filled time in between the spectacles. From August 17 to 23, everything—including parking—was free.[8]

As this Chicago Park District water show was splashing through its ambitious agenda, a harbinger of things to come kicked off at the tiny Curtiss-Reynolds Airport in northwest suburban Glenview. Flying shows were very popular through the 1930s as the National Air Races in Cleveland,

Ohio, drew crowds and newsreel coverage. Barnstorming acts by individual pilots during the 1920s matured into flights of daredevil aerobatic teams called "Flying Circuses." More reliable planes fostered more daring stunts and entertaining spectacles. On Sunday, August 17, 1936, the Chicago Girls Flying Club began a ten-event air show. That Sunday evening, while the young girls in swimsuits were regally towed across Burnham Lagoon to smile for photographers, other young ladies were wiping the oil off their goggles and changing the sparkplugs in their radial engines after a day of stunting in the clouds. Many changes were coming.

Entry into World War II helped rescue the United States economy. The American ability to create corporate organizations and achieve mass production of high-quality goods saved it from becoming a technological also-ran. The war forced the creation of innovative aircraft and solutions that carried over into civilian use.

Chicago continued to grow as a commercial aviation center. Orchard Field, northwest of the city, had boomed in size and importance during the war as Douglas Aviation built a plant next to its runways producing C-54 cargo aircraft. At the war's end, the airport was renamed after navy ace "Butch" O'Hare, who shot down five Japanese fighter planes in one combat mission. Municipal Airport also owed its new name to the war, as it was rechristened Midway after the battle in the Pacific that turned the tide of the conflict in that theatre.

Off Chicago's Lake Michigan coast, the wartime effort put on a regular "air and water" show as twin flattops landed and launched bomber and fighter planes. In August 1942, the USS *Wolverine* (IX-64) was commissioned by the U.S. Navy as a training aircraft carrier for navy and marine pilots destined for action in the Pacific war. A year later, the USS *Sable* (IX-81) joined its sister ship, and both were docked just south of the Chicago Municipal Pier. Because of this wartime service, the name was changed to Navy Pier. What distinguished these two vessels—called the "Cornfield Fleet"—from the U.S. Navy was the fact that both started life as coal-fired, side-wheel paddle steamers. The *Wolverine* began as the *Greater Buffalo* in 1924, and the Cleveland and Buffalo Transit Company had christened the *Sable* the *Seeandbee* in 1913 as an elegant lake passenger cruiser. When war was declared, the upper deck amenities of both boats (there are no "ships" in the Great Lakes) were scraped off, and 550-foot aircraft landing decks were laid. This was a shorter deck than on fleet carriers, so the thinking went, if the pilots could put a combat plane onto the side-wheeler's deck, they could land on any other deck.

The paddle-wheel lake steamer SS *Greater Buffalo* was converted into the USS *Sable* in the 1940s, a navy training flattop for future pilots. Chicagoans saw daily air shows as navy war planes learned to land and take off on the carrier—or crash into the lake to be plucked out by waiting boats. *Courtesy Glenview Naval Air Station Museum.*

Aviation Legacy Shines through the Great Depression

The side-wheel, coal-fired paddle steamer SS *Greater Buffalo* during a Great Lakes cruise. The boat would be yanked from retirement for the World War II wartime effort. *Courtesy Glenview Naval Air Station Museum.*

Opposite, bottom: The former lake steamers as training aircraft carriers USS *Wolverine* and USS *Sable* berthed on the south side of Navy Pier during World War II. *Courtesy Glenview Naval Air Station Museum.*

During operations, every morning the two vessels would cast off from Municipal Pier, their side-wheels thrashing the water and coal smoke belching from their funnels. Topside, there were no elevators to raise and lower planes to below-deck storage. The aircraft flew in squadrons from the Glenview Naval Air Station and practiced their landings and takeoffs or touch-and-go passes.

Chicagoans were fascinated by the constant parade of navy and marine aircraft snarling above the city as the planes formed to make their assigned runs on the carriers. All totaled, the air fleet training exercises involved more than 200 lost aircraft in 126 accidents. The tally includes: 41 TBM/TBF Avengers, 1 F4U Corsair, 38 SBD Dauntless, 4 F6F Hellcats, 17 SNJ Texans, 2 SB2U Vindicators, 37 FM/F4F Wildcats and 3 experimental drones known as TDNs. The latter were "Torpedo Drones," built by the Naval Aircraft Factory. This mostly plywood, remote-controlled, un-manned bomber could carry up to two thousand pounds of explosive ordnance at a speed of 175 miles per hour. About 114 were built. It is an ancestor of today's Predator remote-controlled weapons platform.

This mix of military aircraft flying as individuals and in formations kept plane-spotter hobbyists and lunchtime grass-sitters busy along Chicago's lakefront. At the end of each day, the two aircraft carriers thrashed their way back to Municipal Pier, their decks often littered with broken airplanes being returned for recycling when possible. One of the pilots who wrung out his TBF Avenger torpedo bomber above Chicago and Lake Michigan was future president George Herbert Walker Bush. He was one of the thirty-five thousand pilots who qualified during 120,000 successful landings at the cost of eight pilots killed. And the navy stokers below decks—the "black gang"—who kept coal blazing and steam flowing to the antique paddle wheels of the world's two largest side-wheel steamers deserve credit for helping win the war. On November 11, 1945, the *Wolverine* and *Sable* were decommissioned and sent off to be scrapped. The show was over.

CHAPTER 3

1959–1964

CHICAGO HAS ITS UPS AND DOWNS...AND UPS

By the end of the 1950s, Chicago was firmly entrenched as a business giant in the Midwest. Its rail, air and highway transportation capabilities justified its number-one ranking. The city's hard-work ethic demanded time to relax and play. For the fun side of life, Chicagoans picked their way through to the roller coaster year of 1959.

The Chicago Cardinals, our "other" professional football team, experienced yet another slump, finishing the season with a dismal 2-10 record. The owner, Violet Bidwell, looked back at the preceding few years of mediocre performance and offered the franchise to St. Louis. The team that had started life back in 1898 as an Irish pick-up squad from the South Side went away, leaving the town to pin its remaining hopes on the Chicago Bears.

But if football was circling the drain, baseball fans were ecstatic, at least on Chicago's South Side. The rafters at Comiskey Park rocked as the Chicago White Sox—the "Go-go Sox"—won the American League Pennant. Al Benedict, the Lake Shore Park supervisor, was with Fire Commissioner Robert J. Quinn at the Lake Shore Club across the street from the swimming pool. After the third out in the ninth inning of the final game of the regular season, according to Rudy Malnati, who was Benedict's young shadow at that time, the pair left the club and crossed the street to the park. There, Quinn celebrated the event with a phone call ordering the air raid sirens blown throughout the city. With the Cold War a frigid reality and the threat of Soviet ICBM missiles hanging over every major city in the United States,

Time magazine featured Queen Elizabeth II's trip to Chicago to commemorate the opening of trade via the St. Lawrence Seaway. *Courtesy* Time *magazine archives.*

panic ensued in the neighborhoods. Order was quickly restored, and Quinn's gesture was taken to task in the press.

July brought Chicago into the international scene with a rush. As *Time* magazine reported:

> *This was a celebration of Chicago as a world seaport with the opening of the St. Lawrence Seaway. Countries from all over the world shipped thousands of products to put on display and the main event was the visit to Chicago by Queen Elizabeth II and Prince Philip. They sailed down the new seaway in the* Britannia *royal yacht. It was the first time in history that a reigning British monarch had come to Chicago.*[9]

At least a million Chicagoans lined their Lake Michigan shore as warships escorted the *Britannia* into the yacht harbor, which was packed with at least five hundred private boats, and everything on the water filled the air with shrill horns, bells and whistles. A pair of Chinese junks added to the naval exotica as army and navy jet aircraft whistled and boomed above the scene. Into the sky blazed aerial torpedoes and assorted fireworks, while Chicago's fireboats directed streams of lake water in arcing plumes. On shore, the majestic Buckingham Fountain matched the water show with cascades of its own. According to the royal party, the Windy City welcome was by far the warmest reception it had received in its North American tour.

Two thousand Chicago police failed to contain the surging crowds anxious to glimpse the young queen and Prince Philip. "Hey, Liz!" called out some well-wishers, and another more formal hail—"Hey, Queen!"—caused virtual apoplexy in the more protocol-oriented Anglophiles but produced tolerant laughter and waves from the royal couple. Prince Philip enjoyed himself hugely amidst the crowd's exuberance, complimenting one embattled police officer's wood baton, "That's a lovely billy [club]. I'd love to borrow it sometime!"

For fourteen hours, the royal couple was fêted by the city's best midwestern hospitality, including a gold-service, sit-down dinner that evening before their departure. The celebration of the opening of a new international trade port was a great success and proved to be an entertainment high point for all Chicago's citizens, who had a collective love affair with Britain's royals. Following the party's nighttime departure beneath a blaze of lights and fireworks to its waiting yacht, the shoreline opposite Buckingham Fountain was renamed the Queen's Landing. Eventually, $19 million was spent on concrete and decoration to embellish the location.[10]

The summer of 1959 was a cooker, heating up into the nineties week after week. Fate had dropped an apparent windfall in the city's lap when Cleveland was forced to renege on hosting the Third Pan American Games, held for the first time outside a Latin American country. Chicago was the fallback host and scurried about to prepare for the arrival of hundreds of athletes, trainers, coaches and whatever idiosyncratic requirement went with each team's regimen. All did not go well.

Due to the warm summer, the parks were experiencing the heaviest use in their history, and personnel were stretched thin. "Everyone from park superintendent George Donoghue on down is important when it comes to working with the Pan Am Games in addition to our regular schedule," said Director of Special Events Erwin Weiner.

By late August, another batch of two hundred athletes arrived, and six more flags were raised in front of the makeshift Pan American Village. Unfortunately, a collection of American VIPs was scheduled a day too early to witness the raising of Old Glory, and they sweated in the sun for a long time before they were told to come back the next day. The heat also caused problems at the Portage Park swimming pool. Robert Black, the Park District chief engineer, was faced with sizzling eighty-three-degree water when international competition called for a sixty-nine- to seventy-three-degree optimum temperature. He pondered whether to dump ice into the pool or pump in fresh water.

Not that the Brazilian swim team was concerned with water temperature; it had been sent to practice at the soccer field. The Brazilian soccer team, meanwhile, assembled in confusion at the edge of the warm swimming pool. The Brazilians were at least in the city. U.S. Customs in Miami had ambushed the Peruvian shooting team and impounded its weapons. Seventeen members of the women's track and basketball teams also registered a complaint as scrambled reservations crammed them all into one room at their "village" in the Shoreland Hotel. Ultimately, the snafus were sorted out, and the games were successfully completed. But the summer ground on.

Almost overlooked amid the August chaos was a local event, a Family Day held in Lake Shore Park, a patch of green managed by the Chicago Park District and connected to a shallow strip of cement-filled Lake Michigan shore by an underground ramp beneath Lake Shore Drive. Restaurateur and driving force overseeing the current Air and Water Show Rudy Malnati remembers:

> *I got involved because I lived near Lake Shore Park. My parents owned* [the restaurants] *Pizzeria Uno and Due and Su Casa, so I started going to the park when I was five. It was a lot different than it is now. I could just go to the park and became one of the kids at the park—involved in the gymnastic program and things of that nature.*

It was there that Rudy met Al Benedict, the Lake Shore Park supervisor. Al had begun his career with the Chicago Park District as a lifeguard perched in a high chair on a Chicago beach. From there, he became a physical education instructor at Chase Park and eventually rose to park supervisor.

"Al was a terrific diver," Rudy says.

> *He was very dynamic and innovative. He started the marathon in Chicago. However, our version was called the Turkey Trot. It was a 4K run held on the Thanksgiving holiday, and the winners got turkeys. Al came up with "Dragboat Races" using speedboats in the Park District Lagoon, and he was the guy who started our Winter Carnivals.*

The water show was the big draw in the early years, often featuring speedboat races. *Courtesy Chicago Park District.*

The hot summer of 1959 called for an event that would be refreshing and involve Chicago kids and their parents. The Park District had begun a program of summer day camps that let kids sign up for different sports and learn from experienced players and coaches. Al Benedict's Lake Shore Park sat at the border of the famed Streeterville section of the city, where, in the nineteenth century, local character "Cap" Streeter had declared his patch of squatter land as sovereign territory. That "patch" had been nothing more than a sand spit then, but later it became a high-rent district cut off from the lake by the multilane Lake Shore Drive. By 1959, the ramp under the drive let park visitors spill on down to the breezes and waves of the lakeshore.

Benedict's idea for a family day had to include the lake, and because of the crush of summer crowds and the Pan American Games stretching Chicago Police Department personnel thin, making the show happen pretty much fell on his shoulders. As Rudy recalls:

The show was titled the Lakeshore Park Air and Water Show and was a part of a Family Day celebration for children enrolled in the Chicago Park District's

The diving exhibition at a 1960s Lake Shore Park show. *Courtesy Chicago Park District.*

day camp program. The budget was eighty-eight dollars, and the show featured a Coast Guard air-sea rescue demonstration (with their HUS-1G Seahorse helicopter), water-skiers, a water ballet, games and a diving competition. We had a big barge put out with a diving board on it, and we had a watermelon-eating contest and a greased pole the kids had to try and climb.

So everyone enjoyed a family day at the beach, and the kids went home happy and suntanned, with pole grease in odd places and watermelon pits in their hair. The Coast Guard buzzed back to its base at the Glenview Naval Air Station, and the crowds of sun-baked parents filed beneath Lake Shore Drive to their cars parked in the ball field or the Old Armory building. They boarded the No. 66 bus or kept walking down Chicago Avenue to the elevated train station.

From that afternoon in August 1959 was born the free public Air and Water Show that continues after more than fifty years.

If Chicago's event planners have learned anything over the years, it is "don't tamper with success." While the 1959 Lake Shore Park Air and Water Show was virtually overlooked in the press, Al Benedict and his staff were determined to lure some free ink from the newspapers in 1960. They did it with sex. Display a pretty girl in a bathing suit on a sunny day at the beach and you have a story and a photo op if the news is slow that day.

On August 4, 1960, the *Chicago Tribune* stripped in a City News Bureau story that read, "5 Seek Title of Mermaid Queen Sunday." It followed that enticement with: "five south side girls will compete at 2 p.m. Sunday for the title of Mermaid Queen of the Lake Shore Park water show at Chicago Avenue and the lake." Fifteen queen contestants were ferried aboard one of the Chinese junks (sent over from Hong Kong to greet Queen Elizabeth in 1959) to the show barge anchored just off the lakefront. Park District commissioner William L. McFetridge crowned the winner from the pre-selected five finalists.

As the flashbulbs popped and the young women were sailed away, the constant water-show entertainment resumed. The Chain O' Lakes Boat Club launched twenty-five ski boats, each capable of speeds up to one hundred miles per hour. They roared past, sending up plumes of spray, to be followed by a more sedate, but no less competitive, race featuring Sea Scouts piloting their cutters with ten scouts manning the sails and lines of each twenty-seven-foot craft.

In between these sailing and boat handling demonstrations, swimmers, divers and synchronized water ballet performers churned through the cold lake waves. While everyone's attention was drawn down to the choppy lake, the show announcer called out a special presentation from the Troop Carrier Command stationed at O'Hare Field, and down the lakefront came a flight of the famous C-119 "Flying Boxcars."

These C-119G cargo carriers loomed huge above the spectators as the planes pounded past, their thirty-five-hundred-horsepower Wright Cyclone piston engines throttled back from their almost three-hundred-mile-per-hour top speed. Beneath and behind the cockpit hung the enormous cargo hull with its rear-loading doors. The roar of the engines reverberated off the buildings, and the air force workhorses began a slow bank out over the lake to make another pass before climbing for altitude and churning their way back to O'Hare Field.

There were no acrobatics or breathtaking stunts, just a flyby of American air power. But the fact that the planes were there for *them*, the spectators, brought forth the cheers and applause. Most people in the audience had never seen the big planes up close, and now twenty thousand Chicagoans

Chicago Police Department lifeboats on duty at Lake Shore Park in the 1960s. *Courtesy Chicago Park District.*

could feel the engine growls vibrate against their bodies. It was a moment not lost on the event organizers.

By 1961, the Lake Shore Park Water Show had become a "Third Annual" event in the press, and once again fifteen beauties selected to compete in the Miss Mermaid judging led off the festivities. The production began at 2:00 p.m. on July 23. The following month, lakefront festivities also included the enduring "Venetian Night," begun in 1958 at the request of Mayor Richard J. Daley for a parade of decorated boats. The Chicago Yachting Association stepped up and created the parade as a nighttime extravaganza featuring the glitterati of the sailing scene slowly motoring their boats from Roosevelt Road to Monroe Street. Lights and displays, as well as costumed hunky crewmen and bathing-suited crewwomen, were lavishly splashed about the chrome and white work. When it began, the theme was a night in Venice, but after that, numerous themes from "Famous Films" to "Elvis" have adorned the boats.

Chicagoans found viewing points in the grass along that stretch of lakefront from the grassy slopes of the Adler Planetarium on the south shore

The Chicago Fire Department performs its air-rescue demonstration for a 1960s audience. *Courtesy Chicago Park District.*

to the gala-decorated Chicago Yacht Club up near Monroe Street. It is a posh and exclusive scene, showing off considerable sums of money spent in gilding Chicago's yachting fleet. For the shore watchers, it is a night of fantasy, not unlike the populace watching gold-encrusted carriages rumbling down the cobblestone streets and through the gates of Versailles.

If Venetian Night was the aquatic equivalent of flaunting it, then the Lake Shore Park Water Show was, and is, the festival for *the rest of us*. The spectator price is the same, but at the water show those were the neighborhood kids out there on the barge, diving, tumbling, strutting in a swimsuit and hammering a ski boat through the wave chop. There were kids showing water-rescue techniques and demonstrating that there's more to being a Sea Scout than learning to tie knots. Even though the participants mostly came from the well-heeled avenues of Streeterville, the Gold Coast and the North Shore—it *seemed* more casual and homespun.

In 1961, the navy provided the "air" portion of the show, hauling "victims" clear of the waves with slings and rising above a crowd still enamored with the rarity of a live hovering helicopter. In five years or so, Vietnam would stifle that wonder, as the *wup-wup-wup* of Huey gunships became a staple of the evening TV news. But in that summer of 1961, the announcer had no trouble bringing an appreciative cheer from the audience.

In addition to four classes of racing hydroplanes skimming across the water, leaving rooster tails of spray in their wake, the stately fireboat *Victor Schlaeger* cruised past, filling the air with colored jets from its pump-driven water guns fore and aft. In a few short years, the Chicago lakefront had become an up-close showplace, a stage for its citizens unrivaled anywhere. South of Lake Shore Park and the Venetian Night parade ground, a new convention center—McCormick Place—had risen. This great slab of a building costing $35 million and offering over 300,000 square feet of display space opened and hosted the 1961 Automobile Show. It was a monumental construction, inscribed with bas-relief in vertical panels of stone and open to the lake in wide sweeping terraces. It invited the rest of the country and the world to Chicago. In architecture, art, music, commerce and entertainment, the city had matured beyond the limited expectations of flyover country. It was now thinking big.

By 1962, the small Family Day of 1959 had matured into a much grander concept. It still offered the hometown touch of the Miss Chicago Mermaid beauty contest, won by Miss Kay Hamlander, age nineteen, who had been voted Miss North Avenue Beach.[11] The Chain O' Lakes Boat Club still came through with a variety of roaring, splashing aquatic events. But a new note was added, and the water show truly became the *Air* and Water Show.

Following one of the previous shows, a sixteen-year-old staff member, Marty Welfeld, suggested to Al Benedict, "Why not bring the Air Force Thunderbirds and the Army Golden Knights here?" To this ambitious offer, Al said, "Sure, kid. If you think you can pull that off, go ahead."[12] On August 5, 1962, when the air force announcer boomed into his microphone, "Ladies and Gentlemen, the United States Air Force Thunderbirds!" thousands of Chicagoans could hardly believe the explosion of sound and speed that signaled the arrival of six F-100 Super Sabre jet fighters in bright silver livery. The smoke-trailing Delta formation split into a four-plane diamond as two F-100 "Huns" peeled away to become solo performers.

For the entire performance, the six fighters climbed, dived, banked, flew straight up, flew inverted and made what appeared to be suicidal opposing passes by the solo pilots. The F-100 was the first U.S. military fighter capable of breaking the sound barrier, but the FAA had ruled against the practice

The Thunderbirds entertained in 1962 as this solo jet passed behind the Lake Shore Park diving barge. *Courtesy Chicago Park District.*

because of possible damage to civilian property from the sonic boom. Still, at one hundred feet, ripping across the lakefront skyline, flashing above the armada of sailboats, motorboats and the stage barge, the jets' afterburner push when they lit it off sent a pressure wave that got everyone's attention like a fist against the chest.

And if jet fighter aircraft tearing up the sky in front of Lake Shore Park wasn't up-close action enough for the audience, the U.S. Army provided in-your-lap excitement. Thousands of feet above the city, a De Havilland DH-2C Beaver aircraft seemed to hang suspended on its single propeller as the jumpmaster watched a test streamer float down toward the strip of shore between Lake Michigan and the wall of buildings surrounding a tiny patch of green. Frigid air blasted in through the open side door as the pilot banked through a turn to repeat the run across the drop zone. In the fuselage of the plane waited the Golden Knights—the Strategic Army Corps Sport Parachute Team—the conceptual creation of Brigadier General Joseph Stilwell.

Assembled to go head to head against the Soviet Union's sport parachute teams dominating international competition, the team of thirteen military

The U.S. Army Golden Knights always dropped in with flags or smoke flares tied to their ankles. *Courtesy Chicago Park District.*

parachutists was formally organized in 1959. On June 1, 1961, they became the army's official aerial demonstration unit. Their job, besides representing the United States in international competitions, was to motivate young men and women into the recruiting offices across the country. On this day, the jumpmaster stood in the wide door looking down toward several thousand

The Blue Angels F9F-8T jet used for press orientation flights as experienced by the author. *Courtesy Naval Aviation Museum, Pensacola, FL.*

people who were little more than a colorful stain between the lake and the land. They, in turn, strained to see the small droning spec in the sky where his team waited.

The turn finished, the high-wing transport made its final run. Buffeted by the wind, the "stick" of jumpers stood in single file. Green light. Out the door in a rush, the men launched into the prop blast, followed last by the jumpmaster. Arms and legs spread, they dropped. Each suit had an automatic air pressure release that would spill out the main chute at a safe altitude even if—for whatever reason—the D-ring was not pulled. Wind rippled their jumpsuits and beat against their faces and goggles as their velocity reached 150 feet per second. They maneuvered individually but remained a cohesive unit as the buildings reached up and the mass of people became individual faces. The paratroopers would land "wet" because of the small target offered by the stage barge. Their chutes were standard-issue parachutes except for moveable panels that allowed for more precise steering than just hauling on the risers to tip the canopy and to hold and dump air. And then Lake Michigan greeted them. As they plunged beneath the surface, they punched their harness releases to free themselves from the lines and chutes to tread

THE AUTHOR AND THE BLUE ANGELS

At the Marine Corps Air Station in Yuma, Arizona, a tech sergeant leaned into the cockpit of the F9F-8T Cougar.

"Listen up," he barked as he fastened my five-point harness. "Sir, do you see that handle in the floor between your legs? Yes, that one. If the commander tells you to eject, you do not say 'What?' You do not say 'Huh?' You do not say 'Now?' You reach down and pull up on that handle. That action arms a 105mm artillery shell under your ass. Next, you reach up and behind your helmet and grasp this curtain edge. Feel that? Good. Pull it down sharply as far as it will go. That sets the timer and even God cannot stop it from blowing you and your seat through the canopy, clear of the tail and up into the blue yonder. Do not look to the commander for help, because he will already be gone. If your chute does not open, you can apply for a refund from the quartermaster. Do you understand, sir?"

I understood. I listened to the whine build as the pilot ran up the engine and released the brakes. As we rolled toward the runway, the whine became thunder. I was sucked back in my seat. The nose pointed at the sky, and the desert dropped away as though it had fallen off a cliff. The sky turned from blue to purple as the altimeter wound up, and a chill suffused through the metal even though the sun scalded the perspex canopy. The commander pushed the nose over in a graduated arc, and my body tried to float up against the harness restraint. My camera did float up off my lap, as did my tape recorder. Droplets of water—silver globules—floated up past my helmet visor, leftovers from when the inside of the canopy was last washed. We were weightless at zero G. The wonder of it! And then everything came back down.

The desert, mountains and cantaloupe fields, and the black tracery of the air station runways far below, snapped into frame. We hurtled toward the ground. There was no sense of speed except for the altimeter spinning in the opposite direction and

water in their inflating life vests until the pick-up boats collected them and their gear. Through the sloshing water, hails from the boats and the thump of oars came the cheers and clapping for another successful show by the parachute team from Fort Bragg, North Carolina.

In 1964, the Lake Shore Park Air and Water Show really hit its stride and never looked back. This time, though, one act did not quite hit its mark. A ten-man team of experienced jumpers of the famed 101st Airborne Division, the "Screaming Eagles," launched themselves into the azure sky ten thousand feet above Chicago. Each man with a minimum of three thousand jumps had been warned of a thirteen-knot wind at ground level and had bailed out early to allow for drift above the *details beginning to appear in the beige landscape. The control stick between my legs came back toward me, and as it did, the pressure climbed. I couldn't raise my forearms off my thighs. Invisible fingers clawed at my cheeks, pulling down the skin. My vision began to tunnel in from the sides to a red film, a gray film. We came level, and my arms worked again. In a few blinks, my eyes functioned once more.*

Author Gerry Souter takes a flight with the Blue Angels in 1964 at Yuma, Arizona, where the team was rehearsing for a program. *Gerry Souter Collection.*

"Sorry about that," the commander apologized. "Wasn't supposed to go above four Gs, but we touched six. You okay?"

"Roger that," I rasped, trying to stay with the vernacular.

After a routine of rolls, loops and head-snapping turns, he took us down, and it was over too soon. I transitioned to the Chicago Tribune *a few months later, in time to watch "the Blues" erupt above my hometown lakeshore, taking my memories with them.*[13]

Olive Park filtration plant just north of Navy Pier. The big wind never materialized. Reminiscent of their scattered ordeal above Normandy in 1944, the 101st jumpers splashed down as close as fifteen feet from the barge stage to a distant two hundred yards away. Lifeguard boats standing by poured on the coal to reach the thrashing parachutists bobbing in the frigid water.

"Man, that Lake Michigan was the coldest lake I've ever been in," remarked Sergeant Michael Kremar, arriving sodden and shivering to good-natured applause.[14]

That year, the navy performed more than extracting damp "victims" from the lake beneath the whirling blades of its Glenview-based helicopter. Blue and gold shot across the crowded shore in a blur of screaming F-11F-1 jet fighters as the Blue Angels arrived. The supersonic aircraft split into their solo and diamond formations above the thousands of upturned faces that now spilled across both Oak Street Beach to the north and North Avenue Beach farther north into Lincoln Park.

CHAPTER 4

BIGGER AND BETTER

CREATING A TRADITION

Four girls in fashionable swimsuits waited near the Ohio Street boat ramp. Their chaperones fussed about, looked at their watches and chatted with the show volunteers. The sun beat down on the pavement, and Lake Michigan waves caressed its concrete slope. The whine of a car engine announced the arrival of their ride in the procession that would wind past thousands of Lake Shore Park spectators and the masses of people that now spilled north and south of the park's concrete shoreline.

Even allowing for the boxy standards of mid- to late 1960s auto design, the small white convertible that drove up from the parking lot was a punky little car. The girls knew what to expect but were still apprehensive as they climbed into the vehicle. It had fashionably hooded headlights, a raked windscreen and straight-line fenders that harkened back to the omnipresent Detroit-type fins. What made it appear even the slightest bit odd was its height above the ramp. The entourage filed in and, with more than casual care, slammed shut the two doors.

With a nudge from the rear-mounted forty-three horsepower British Triumph engine, the strange vehicle inched forward. Three of the beauty queens grabbed handholds to steady themselves and settled along the top of the backseat, while the fourth rode shotgun next to the driver.

With a forward shove of a transmission lever, the two-speed gears engaged, and two nylon propellers below and beneath the car's rear end began to spin. The car drove down the ramp and into the lake. Water gurgled past the sealed doors and then halfway up the sides until the slightly V-shaped fairings

The unique Amphicar, bedecked with fair beauties vying for the Miss Mermaid crown, was a feature at the Air and Water Show. *Courtesy Chicago Park District.*

at the front began to push the lake aside. At a stately seven miles an hour, the Amphicar motored forward and then slewed right as the driver turned the steering wheel in that direction. The front wheels became rudders. Still a bit rigid with apprehension, the girls waved to those they left behind on shore and put on their best faces for the waiting Air and Water Show crowd.

The Amphicar Model 770 was a German amphibious novelty that worked surprisingly well with a two-speed transmission for water navigation and a four-speed that allowed seventy miles per hour on the expressway. It began to turn up on the coasts and inland waterways until the EPA and DOT regulations went into effect. The Amphicar was the trick ride of choice for parading beauty queens down Chicago's waterfront in 1965. By the time the plant shut down in 1968, both the novelty and demand had worn off, and U.S. environmental protection regulations had closed out the amphibious car's American market.[15]

Inspired by the success of both the Lake Shore Park Air and Water Show and the regal Venetian Night, Mayor Richard J. Daley decided that the exploitation of Chicago's front yard needed a real showman's touch. For 1966, the two-day production was merged with Venetian Night, and a week of events was scattered along practically the entire shore in Chicago's first Lakefront Festival.

For the next few years, virtually every newspaper story about the Lakefront Festival began with "King Neptune rose out of the waters of Lake Michigan." A member of the Lake Michigan Yachting Association, or someone involved in the yachting scene, usually portrayed the "King." In 1966, Martin Roefer of Wadsworth, Illinois, was wrapped in the ceremonial Greek god–like toga with a seaweed-curls wig and carrying a rather deadly appearing trident. He arrived dry-shod on the lakefront at Balbo Drive to be greeted by Mayor Daley. Voted "Yachtsman of the Year," Roefer proceeded across Grant Park to State Street, where he "took control of the city" and led a parade of floats, marching bands and general hoopla for spectators who lined the route. The baton twirlers, military units, drum and bugle corps and decorated horses followed the festival queen, Miss Joan Conrath, age nineteen, and her court with great enthusiasm for the hour-long extravaganza.[16]

The festival kicked off with 150,000 Chicagoans and tourists lining the shore from Monroe Street south to the Adler Planetarium for the ninth annual Venetian Night. Just prior to the boat parade, a water-ski show groped its way though a rushed performance in near darkness. When the sun had dipped behind the wall of downtown skyscrapers, the audience gazed with envious eyes on the parade of conspicuous consumption and dazzling displays as forty boats made their stately way north through the harbor. At their head was King Neptune, clutching his trident and smiling with fatherly affection at Miss Conrath. As the last of the yachting set slid past, a blast of fireworks lit up the sky, ending the festivities and beginning the long traffic jam home. According to the Chicago press, the night was "magical."

But that day of parades was only the beginning of a fun-filled week engineered by the director of Mayor Daley's special events, Colonel Jack Reilly. The "Colonel" was Daley's paladin and a loyal friend of the family. He also had the ability to elbow his way into any city hall photo-op and knew everyone who was anyone by their first name, unless they crossed him or failed to live up to his grandiose expectations. The offenders were promptly banished from his Rolodex and constantly churning press release mill. Where Daley was insecure and stiff, Reilly was the glad-hander and back-slapper. He was also the engineer and enthusiastic megaphone mouthpiece of the Lakefront Festival.

A genuine bevy of bathing beauties adorns this yacht as it passes an appreciative 1970s audience at Lake Shore Park. *Courtesy Chicago Park District.*

In 1966, the eighth annual Chicago Park District Lake Shore Air and Water Show at Chicago Avenue became integrated into the weeklong package. It existed "in conjunction with" the Lakefront Festival. Al Benedict remained its director and predicted, "Given the favorable weather, it will be the best show ever." But it was Colonel Reilly who jumped in with reassurances when the Golden Knights met with gusty winds and a choppy lake as they drifted past the landing zone to their soggy splashdown.

Benedict and his staff continued to deliver top entertainment for two days. Besides the Blue Angels racing around the lakefront in their F11F-1 Tiger jets, the 126th Air Refueling Wing of the Illinois Air National Guard sent a KC-135 tanker to refuel a pair of USAF jet fighters at an altitude of only five hundred feet above the water. This year, however, not all of the flying was composed of military or tactical maneuvers spiced up with proximity—not when the "Flying Professor" hove into view above the heads of the surprised crowd.

Captain Richard A. Schram had almost a quarter century of piloting and engineering behind him when he appeared in the 1966 Air and Water Show.

Above: Rudy Malnati as a young man (curly hair) receiving the Golden Knights baton that was passed between jumpers on the way down in the early 1970s. *Courtesy Chicago Park District*.

Below: A KC-135 tanker refueling two Phantom II Vietnam War–era jets in a flyby. *Courtesy Chicago Park District*.

The Flying Professor was a legendary stunt created by Captain Richard A. Schram playing the part of a tipsy civilian who steals an airplane and blunders into the show. Shown here is Schram in full costume with his son. *Courtesy Glenview Naval Air Station Museum.*

His act had been honed to make the easy look difficult and the difficult look impossible. He did not fly a state-of-the art stunt plane designed to corkscrew through the air, nor was his plane particularly "hot" like the scorching jets. He flew a homely Piper Cub—usually borrowed from a local flier. In shows that were staged at airports, he would wander out on the field in top hat and tails, carrying a large book titled *How to Fly*. Like a drunken partygoer, he stumbled into the parked Piper and fooled with the controls while the show announcer begged him to get out of the plane. The engine fired, the prop spun and he took off tilted on one wheel with the wing almost brushing the runway. Hilarity ensued. For the Air and Water Show, he appeared overhead flying sideways and ignoring the pleas of the microphone man. Schram's great acrobatic skill wrung out the little Cub to the edge of disaster, banking, diving, stalling, looping, trying to "regain" control of the plane and taking the crowd with him for twenty minutes.

The Flying Professor was famous throughout the world. Though Schram was a former navy officer, he never took flight training because of the service flight prohibition against married men. However, because of his civilian flying skills, he did receive his wings—one of the few men in history to have that honor. After earning the respect of the military flight demonstration teams, he only flew in U.S. Department of Defense sanctioned events. On June 4, 1969, at age fifty-two, Schram flew his act at Reading, Pennsylvania. His concluding stunt was to stall the plane while climbing straight up and then fall off—rotating around the axis of his tail—in a powered hammerhead stall to point straight down and recover to swoop into a perfect landing. At Reading, he just went straight down and never recovered.[17]

Ninety-mile-per-hour speedboat races once again churned the water in front of Lake Shore Park. Water-skiing demonstrations by Lou Scalise and his water-ski champions sent the spray flying. The thirteen beauty queens putted past the crowd perched on the rear decks of their Amphicars, while the Great Lakes Navy Band pounded out a particularly enthusiastic "Anchors Aweigh."

The 1967 Lakefront Festival suffered from bad weather, and when King Neptune rose from Lake Michigan's depths, he found Mayor Daley waiting for him at city hall instead of the shoreline. At noon on that August 14, Neptune led a float and trailer procession down the Chicago River to Wacker Drive, tramped south to Adams Street and then turned left to city hall. As with the previous festival, events were scattered about the city in profusion, and some included dunking in the Chicago River.

Following swimming races out at Navy Pier and the contest featuring hundreds of young girl baton twirlers spinning away in front of the Civic Center vying for the title of Miss Chicago Majorette, the river became the next venue. Rowing, paddling and speedboat races were scheduled to churn down the river beneath the bridges. A "watercade" of decorated boats

Along Lake Shore Park, calm waters created by an offshore breakwater allowed formation water-skiing in the 1960s and '70s. *Courtesy Chicago Park District.*

added to the riverside festivities. At this time in the evolution of the Chicago River, the quality of its water had been improved considerably, but the idea of actually splashing about in its current could only be received with heroic resignation. In the 1950s, urban myth claimed that Chicago River water was known to dissolve rust off bolts and had a higher acidic content than a bottle of Coca-Cola. In 1967, the federal government had ordered the city to do something about the repeated overflows of solid waste and storm water from the sewers into the river raising its bacteria count to unacceptable levels.[18] The deep tunnel project that solved many of the river's ills would not break ground until 1969.

Venetian Night was scheduled for Friday evening and included a special surprise: two brightly painted and decorated dragon boats, gifts from the Taiwan[19] city of Taipei. They were to take part in the Venetian Night boat parade with men from Chicago's Chinatown at the oars. The boats had arrived on the SS *Fuyu Maru* for transport to Chicago on the Santa Fe Railroad. By the time they arrived, there was not much time to practice before the parade. Each boat was forty-five feet long with a four-foot beam, and each had thirty pairs of oars, two drums and two cymbals. The drums and cymbals were used to keep the cadence of the rowing beat. Of the seventy volunteers from Chinatown, only about thirty had experience with boat oars of any kind.

As the upstaged yachtsmen fretted, a Great Lakes rainstorm sloshed into the city with high winds. The canoe-like, narrow-beam dragon boats were severely pummeled at their moorings and capsized. Both were refloated and towed down to Burnham Harbor to await the weather verdict for the following Friday. Meanwhile, the rain hung around and gave everyone fits for Sunday's Air and Water Show. Fortunately, the Sunday show came off on schedule under partly cloudy skies and a chilly-for-summer seventy-two degrees. The sodden dragon boats performed with distinction.

The Air and Water Show split its venues in 1968. On Saturday, August 10, the show moved to Rainbow Beach between Seventy-fifth and Seventy-eighth Streets on Chicago's South Side. This beach had been expanded in depth over the years from a strip of sand backing onto railroad ties and a gravel walk in the 1940s to a popular playground for the largely Polish, Irish and Jewish South Shore neighborhood by the 1960s. The South Shore's demographic had shifted considerably as African Americans replaced the ethnic groups who headed for new housing developments in the north and south suburbs. With Martin Luther King Jr.'s assassination on April 4, 1968, and the civil rights issue looming large in Chicago and the rest of the country, a more inclusive venue seemed appropriate. At least on Rainbow Beach, the U.S. Army Golden Knights parachute team landed in the sand rather than in the chilled lake.

The changes continued as the show reached its eleventh anniversary in 1969. On August 8, a luncheon was set up for the military personnel who were participating in the program. One of the key fundraisers and supporters of the show, Chicago tycoon David X. Meyers, was helping set up the buffet when *Chicago Tribune* columnist David Condon buttonholed him. Meyers put the show's success in perspective:

> *Lake Michigan is Chicago's greatest natural recreation asset and we're happy to have the cooperation of the Chicago Park District in utilizing its facilities for the water and air show.*
>
> *The Park District is underwriting only a part of the show. We're still chasing dollars for the rest of the financing, so if any of your parishioners has an extra buck, he can send it to Lake Shore Park Water Show, 808*

Shot from above, a circle formation of Golden Knights parachutists drops down on Lake Shore Park in the 1960s and '70s. *Courtesy Chicago Park District.*

Lake Shore Drive, Chicago, 60611. We want a rousing success this year to assure continuation of the show for years to come.

There are two purposes for this show. First of all we want to acquaint more and more Chicagoans with the vast recreational opportunities available on our lakefront. More important, we want them to get the idea that our lakefront is worth preserving. We think that when they realize how important the lakefront is, they'll enlist in the war on pollution too. Chicago is a very lucky town and I hope that after Sunday's show, another 500,000 citizens will be determined to "save our lake."[20]

Over August 9 and 10, 1969, the show was once again split to fly over Rainbow Beach on Saturday and Lake Shore Park on Sunday. The big change for that year was the shift away from the Blue Angels and Air Force Thunderbirds to the U.S. Naval Reserve Flight Demonstration Team, the Air Barons. While the navy still promoted the Blue Angels, it sanctioned the Air Barons in 1969 to show that the naval reserve could also field a tight

CHICAGO PARK DISTRICT
Department of Recreation

11th Annual   **LAKE SHORE PARK**

AIR & WATER THRILL SHOW

Air Barons - Tactical Jet Flight
Demonstration Team, U.S. Navy
Golden Knights
U.S. Army Parachute Team
U.S. Navy Underwater Demolition Team
Nick Rezick - Stunt Pilot
"Scully's" Water Ski Champions
Speedboat Races - Ed Zender, Announcer
Beauty Queens
Helicopter Trapeze Artist
5th Army Band

SUNDAY, AUGUST 10, 1969 • 2 P.M.
CHICAGO AVE. AT THE LAKE

Free   *Free*

REACH OUT ▶
☐ RECREATION ☐ EDUCATION ☐ JOBS
CALL 744-3211

An Air Barons poster for the 1969 Air and Water Show, where they performed representing the U.S. Navy Reserve in A4 Skyhawk jet fighters. *Courtesy Terry Denton Collection.*

The Air Barons of the U.S. Navy Reserve fly over Lake Shore Park in their diamond formation. *Courtesy Terry Denton Collection.*

group of combat-ready pilots flying state-of-the-art supersonic aircraft. The A4 Skyhawk was the lightest, smallest dog-fighting jet in the U.S. arsenal, but in its later generations, with a hot hand on the stick, it was a match for any other combat jet. Skyhawks were used as aggressor aircraft to test the capabilities of navy pilots in aerial combat at the famous Top Gun school. Many a hotshot F-14 Tomcat pilot had his six waxed by the fast and nimble "enemy" Skyhawks.

The six "weekend warriors" staged out of Naval Air Station, Glenview, so participation in the Chicago show was just a nice flight over the lake in front of a hometown crowd. The pilots included a trust banker and an art director for *Playboy* magazine among the mix of "day jobs" representing the ready-to-fight force of twenty-nine thousand reservists. Their schedule of shows was national in scope, and they included unique elements in their presentation that set them apart from the other service teams.

In one low and slow pass through the show box, planes five and six performed a crippled plane air-to-air refueling. The lead plane slowed to refuel the trailing aircraft, which was flying "dirty" with wheels and flaps deployed. From an under-wing fuel pod, the lead plane extended (streamed) a drogue hose with a funnel-shape connection on the end. The "crippled" aircraft plugged its fuel filler probe into the drogue to receive fuel.

Above: The Air Barons pose with their Skyhawk aircraft in 1970. *Courtesy Terry Denton Collection.*

Right: The U.S. Navy Reserve Air Barons perform an air-to-air refueling in their A4 Skyhawk jet fighters in 1969 at Lake Shore Park. *Courtesy Terry Denton Collection.*

Their total show lasted about twelve minutes, during which a new maneuver was in front of the crowd about every forty-five seconds. While they performed few relatively risky or high-speed maneuvers, their speed restriction to about 250 knots allowed them maximum tightness in their formations and kept their planes in front of the audience without requiring a mile of space to make a scorching return flight.

Terry Denton, the trust banker/pilot recalled:

> *The show line, while over water, was easy to spot. I recall threading our planes among the skyscrapers, noting how beautiful the city was. The*

downside was the crowd did not see the pilots' routine of marching to our planes, nor were the pilots able to mix with the crowd after the show. The Air Barons were, after all, ambassadors for the navy and PR, and recruiting was the mission.[21]

From a six-plane delta configuration to the four-plane diamond with two solo Skyhawks tearing up the lakefront, the Air Barons performed a great show and proved an effective recruiting tool for the U.S. Navy Reserves.

The Air Barons were invited back in 1970 for—up to that time—the biggest Air and Water Show ever attempted. It literally filled the air with all manner of aircraft following the same legacy as left by the 1911 Aviation Meet, which set such a huge mark to beat.

Before the planes had their moment, a French frigate, the *Commandant Bourdais,* sailed upriver and docked in front of the Merchandise Mart. The French sailors were a curiosity to Chicagoans who toured the vessel. To capitalize on the visit, a contingent of American sailors was marched into line at the Civic Center Plaza for a "hands across the ocean" ceremony. If the international flavor provided by the French on Friday was not enough, the next day found a British strategic delta wing nuclear bomber pounding down the shore of Rainbow Beach.

The Avro Vulcan bomber had achieved its maiden flight in 1952 and served in various capacities—mostly symbolic, like our B-47 and B-36 Cold War "deterrent" weapons. By the 1970s, the plane's role had been diminished by the success of the Allies' nuclear submarine fleets. It became the rock star of the air shows, touring the world and spreading its bat-like wings over countless awe-struck civilian audiences. Near the end of its days, however, the Vulcan was resurrected for one last job. Using four air-to-air refueling tankers, a flight of Vulcan bombers departed from the Ascension Islands, appeared over the Falkland Islands in 1982 and gave Argentine army airfields a liberal pasting. The Vulcans' appearance in the longest bombing raid in history caused the Argentineans to completely revise their fighter deployment.

If the Vulcan bomber was a nod to the modern age strategic bomber keeping the Cold War at bay, then Dick Lybarger's Boeing Stearman Model 75 biplane fitted with a Pratt & Whitney Wasp Jr. R-985 450 horsepower engine was a throwback to the 1930s, when flying was done by the seat of the pilot's pants. Lybarger made his entrance in this hot rod version of the normally 220-horsepower training plane immediately after Lou Scully's water-ski champions finished swooping over ramps and roaring behind their boats locked in pyramids.

Bigger and Better

A motorboat carrying Andy Anderson sped along the waterfront, while above him Dick Lybarger throttled back the big rotary engine of his biplane to a parallel speed. Beneath the big two-seater dangled a trailing wire ladder. The plane came lower. Anderson stood higher, reaching for the ladder's bottom rung. With virtually no forward vision because of the plane's bulbous engine cowling, Lybarger could only see Anderson's outstretched arm beneath the bottom wing. He cut back the throttle, and the ladder dropped just enough for Anderson to make his grab. Success. With legs kicking dramatically, Anderson hauled his slim frame up the rungs until his toes found the ladder. The instant his grip was secure, Lybarger advanced the throttle to offset the additional weight and began to bank away and up from the water and racing boat. The pair roared past the thousands of cheering spectators.

Lybarger brought back his Stearman 450 after the parade of beauty queens for some solo stunting and then returned again after the U.S. Coast Guard Air-Sea Rescue Unit plucked a "victim" from the lake in one of its new Sea Stallion helicopters. This time, Lybarger's biplane was decorated with Miss Patti Deck lashed to a frame on the top wing, arms outstretched. She had just begun wing walking, joining the long tradition of walkers—female and male—dating back to the post–World War I barnstorming years.

Individual stunt pilots included John Gosney in his Ryan Navion low-wing monoplane and Nick Rezich piloting a Travel-Air 4000 biplane. The E-4000 was built by Travel-Air to compete with the swarm of surplus World War I Standards and JN4 "Jennies" that trained U.S. and British pilots. It was a low, wide-body plane—the front seat was wide enough for two passengers—that used bungee cord shock absorbers to land with some security on rough fields. The last Model 4000 planes were built in 1929 and were powered by Wright Whirlwind J-6 five-cylinder engines outputting 165 horsepower and reaching a top speed of 130 miles per hour. Just before the Vulcan bomber made its appearance, Lybarger, Gosney and Rezich made a final bow, flying together as the Polish Air Force. The closing act featured the popular U.S. Navy Reserve Air Barons in their A-4L Skyhawks. This was their final appearance at the Chicago show because their unit was disbanded in 1971—along with a number of reserve squadrons—as the Vietnam War wound down.

For all the boom and zoom of the 1970 production, it was still the silent fliers that, in turn, brought a hush to the lakeshore. As expected, the U.S. Army Golden Knights parachute team made its descent from ten thousand feet. Their sandy landing at Rainbow Beach almost flattened a few of the

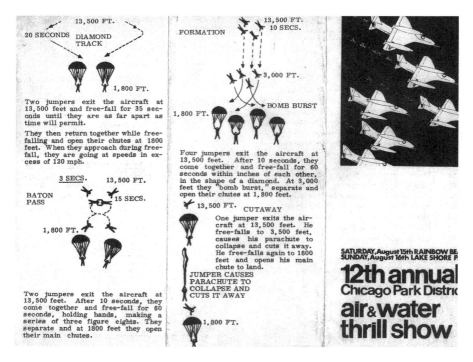

A folded 1970 program for spectators showing the Air Barons' jet aircraft and the Golden Knights' aerial maneuver diagrams. *Courtesy Terry Denton Collection.*

audience members, who scurried to dodge the rain of heavy jump boats caught by a low-altitude wind gust. But this year, the intrusion of a civilian flyer and the relatively new sport of hang gliding had midwesterners staring silently aloft before the Golden Knights made their appearance.

Bill Moyes was an Australian pioneer hang glider and world champion for the years between 1967 and 1973. He built and flew the Moyes Delta Glider designed by John Dickerson. Beneath the Dacron sails supported by aluminum spars and steel bracing, he rode in a Bennett-Moyes harness and trapeze, which had become standard on all hang gliders of the period. The harness permitted the flier to control the attitude and direction of the glider by means of shifting his body while lying beneath the large kite. It was the silence of bird flight that held everyone's attention.

By the time the Chicago Fire Department chugged onto the water stage with its fireboat jetting streams of colored water into the air, the spectators were thoroughly wrung out. The 1970 Air and Water Show had set a high standard for excitement and was a hard act to follow. After

Above: A Golden Knights C-54 jump plane in a pass over Rainbow Beach. *Courtesy Chicago Park District.*

Right: Hang gliding and kite flying were popular air and water sports in the 1970s. *Courtesy Chicago Park District.*

eleven years of these summer events, the size and scope of the show had become huge, requiring more help from donations and volunteers and support from the Chicago Park District. The first 1959 Family Day had a budget of eighty-eight dollars. Now, the list of supporters on the 1970 schedule folder included: Gene's Steak House; George W. Dunne, president of the Cook County Board; Drake Hotel; Holiday Inn; Knickerbocker Hotel; Lake Shore Club; Lake Tower Inn; Pearson Hotel; Sheraton Chicago; Café Brauer; Water Tower Inn; Chicago Fire Department; U.S. Coast Guard; U.S. Navy; U.S. Air Force; U.S. Army;

Lake Shore Park offered a strip of concrete shoreline that followed Lake Shore Drive. *Courtesy Chicago Park District.*

the Mayor of Chicago's Office and all of the independent acts and demonstrations. The budget had climbed into five figures and would only grow as ambitions and expectations also grew.

Bigness had its downside as the city tried to add more sideshows beneath the big top in 1971. The Air and Water Show continued to be one act in a seemingly endless collection of exciting extravaganzas. Like the Caesars in Rome, staging ever more grandiose spectacles in the Coliseum for what the emperors and senate called "the mob," the Lakefront Festival was a giant diversion. While rumors persisted of a cease-fire in Vietnam, the images coming into people's homes on color TV were at odds with the frantically upbeat military assessments issued through the Pentagon. American troops were coming home by the planeload, and "Vietnamization"—handing the hapless South Vietnam army the military hardware with wishes of good luck—was in full swing. The cycle of carpet bombing and returns to the negotiating table had slipped into a pattern that left the Allies with less and less to negotiate each time. At the show site, even the "fun" events had to set aside areas for placard-carrying and bullhorn bloviating demonstrations of antiwar sentiment.

Scheduling the lakefront festivities turned Lake Shore Drive between Ohio Street and North Avenue and the stretch between Madison Street and Pershing Road into a gridlock parking lot as herds of spectators on foot and in cars clogged these arteries. While 110,000 people swarmed into the Loop to watch the return of the Blue Angels and Golden Knights to the Chicago Avenue center stage, farther south at Soldier Field the noisy, frantic Fireman and Police Thrill Show whooped it up to a full house. The usual suspects were also present as King Neptune yet again "rose from the murky depths" of the Chicago River, and the beauty queens were reassured that, regardless of urban myth, Chicago River water would not dissolve their swimsuits.

The international theme was kept alive by a replica of the ship *Nonsuch* sailing under concealed diesel engine power up the river to celebrate the Hudson Bay Colony founders' arrival on the continent three hundred years earlier. Its arrival caused hardcore Cold War warriors to flinch when its crew unlimbered its deck cannon for a few blasts as it approached its moorings. The gunfire reverberating off the Chicago Loop's skyscraper canyon inspired the droll columnist and city Pecksniff Michael Killian to write in his column, "Miami has its hurricanes, San Francisco its earthquakes and Benghazi its locust plagues. But Chicago has its Annual Lakefront Festival."[22]

The layering of superlatives turned the lakefront into a hotbed of giddy stupefaction as speedboats roared down the river, gymnasts pounded the sand at an Oak Street "Beach Meet" and baton twirlers vied with ethnic dancers for crowds. While all this frenetic roaring, twirling and heel pounding dazzled Chicagoans, a track and field meet was in progress, as was a dog-coursing event trotting down the grass in Grant Park. All of this grand hoopla held Chicago's attention as planeloads of army and navy personnel arrived home from Southeast Asia, many of them changing out of their uniforms so they would not by identified as soldiers to be spit upon and called "baby-killers" by antiwar demonstrators who took some time off from the festivities.

Richard Cummings, commodore of the Chicago Yacht Club, wore the toga and King Neptune's wig in 1972 and was greeted by Mayor Daley on one of the water taxi docks along the Chicago River. The taxis had been shut down for the speedboat races, water-skiers and beauty queen parade, causing some grumpy protests from the taxi owners, who lost a chunk of their summer income. But they were drowned out by a fifty-float parade down State Street, rumbling, tooting and booming with marching bands, striding lifeguards in skimpy Speedos, antique cars, stuffed animals, live

The SS *Speedboats* churned up the water at Lake Shore Park for some excitement. *Courtesy Chicago Park District.*

politicians and a horse-drawn trolley followed by a contingent of sweepers from City Streets and Sanitation. Fireworks over Olive Park at the foot of Ohio Street ended the opening activities on August 19.

The river and Loop played host to more events that month with the Thrill Show moving to the Civic Plaza across from city hall. Again, water entertainment rose to the top of the highlights, as did free Park District competitions. The emphasis on participation rather than simple entertainment had become stronger. Swimming, paddling and rowing races churned relentlessly. There are few competitions more difficult to watch, or less spectator-friendly, than long-distance lake swim races.

For the Air and Water segment, the Golden Knights plopped obediently into the chilled lake after their formation flying and baton-passing routines. The USAF Thunderbirds returned to the show that year in their new F4 Phantom jets. After a brief trial with the F-105 Thunderchief in 1963, the "Thuds" turned out to have a lethal structural failure that killed Captain Gene Devlin at Hamilton Air Force Base. They went back to their F-100 Super Sabres until 1969, when the team transitioned to the F-4 Phantom II—the only time in Thunderbird history that they flew the same plane as the Blue Angels, who demonstrated the big jet fighter from 1969 to 1974.

Vietnam-era Blue Angels' F-4J Phantom II fighter-bombers. *Courtesy Naval Aviation Museum, Pensacola, FL.*

The Phantom became the workhorse of U.S. military services in Vietnam. First flown in 1958, the F-4 was originally designed as a single-seat fighter, but as combat requirements were added to its role, the plane became an all-weather interceptor and fighter-bomber, requiring a second crewman or RIO (radar intercept officer). Initially, the plane was a success in the Vietnam theatre, but its armament was restricted to air-to-air missiles. The MiG-17 and, later, MiG-21 North Vietnamese fighters it encountered carried cannon and machine guns, giving them an advantage in a subsonic, close-in dogfight when the Phantom's Sparrow or Sidewinder missiles became impractical. Eventually, a 20mm Vulcan Gatling gun with revolving barrels was added to the F-4.

While the F-4 Phantom II flew with all of the sleek elegance of a flying dump truck, there was a brute strength implied in the plane's ungainly lines, lumps, bumps and extensions. Also, its twin J79 engines' smoky exhaust trails added to its tough-as-nails image. The USAF Thunderbirds switched to the F-4 in 1969, flying without an RIO and using the gun mount space to store colored smoke and the smoke generator. Because the F-4 had been sheathed with metal skin designed to withstand heat generated at twice the speed of sound, a special white paint had to be created for team plane decoration.

The Thunderbirds flew both of their performances above Lake Shore Park in 1972 rather than splitting the events between the original venue and Rainbow Beach on the South Side.

Splashy events held pride of place. Chief among these damp attractions was to be an international fleet spotted into the traditional Friday Venetian Night parade. The entrants included a Venetian gondola, those dragon boats from Taiwan, Irish curraghs, a yakatabune from Japan and a fishing boat sent from Mexico. Unpronounceable exotica included a *Bindalsfaering* from Norway and a homely dory from Nova Scotia. The international theme did not stop at the waterline. Fireworks displays from England, Germany, Japan, Brazil and Italy ended the opening-day gaiety.[23]

But if water was the star of the 1972 Lakefront Festival, it was also the biggest headache. On Wednesday, August 23, a monster boat parade, water-skiers, boat races—all on the Chicago River—plus the not-to-miss Polka Championships held at Buckingham Fountain in Grant Park (Chicago has the largest population of Poles outside of Warsaw) were scheduled. What arrived instead was a great sluicing rain that hammered the city with a Wagnerian display of rumbling thunder and stabs of incandescent lightning dancing among skyscraper rooftops. Down in the river, its surface roiled by pelting raindrops, game boaters and sodden water-skiers pushed off into the sog. Along the concrete riverbanks, about two hundred moist souls huddled beneath umbrellas and folds of disintegrating, ink-bleeding newspapers. Streets became rivers, viaducts became impassable, telephone service failed and residents in the suburb of Hazelcrest watched their basements fill up after a total of more than six inches of ceaseless rain washed down their streets.

At Lake Shore Park from the 1960s to the 1980s, water-skiers were a major feature of the program. *Courtesy Chicago Park District.*

The boat parade chugged on as bilge pumps and bucket bailers worked, while anxious faces peered up into the leaden clouds. Lightning bursts flashed, followed immediately by the hiss, crack and rolling rumble of thunder, signaling another sizzling hit among the rooftop antenna farms. Sadly, despair gripped the Venetian Night planners as the National Weather Service predicted the storms would continue through Friday.

While all this *Sturm und Drang* was pummeling Chicago, the nighttime doings of five arrested burglars in the Democratic National Headquarters at the Watergate Complex in Washington, D.C., were causing ripples that reached out toward the White House. President Nixon, meanwhile, sent more streams of B-52 bombers down the Ho Chi Minh Trail, attempting to hammer the North Vietnamese into submission or back to the negotiating table. In Chicago, tucked away behind sawhorses and edgy policemen, antiwar, anti-Nixon and pro–civil rights demonstrators railed for the TV cameras.

In 1973, a complex series of events brought needed relief from the daily headlines. On January 27, in a ballroom of the Majestic Hotel in Paris, the official delegations of the United States and North Vietnam signed the Paris Peace Accords. This act followed President Nixon's announcement on January 15 of the suspension of offensive actions against North Vietnam, finally ending the longest war in United States history up to that time. If that was good news for the divided country, bad news quickly followed. Problems in the Middle East caused OPEC (Organization of Petroleum Exporting Countries) to double the price of oil sold to the United States. This had the effect of eventually quadrupling the price of gasoline, which caused 20 percent of the nation's gas stations to dry up during the last week of February 1974, according to the American Automobile Association. Travel by car became a gut-wrenching calculation of time, distance and tank capacity as severe rationing went into effect. Long lines formed at gas stations. The huge gas-guzzler cars of the time became liabilities as they swilled down the ethyl. This "oil shock" had the additional effect of encouraging the stock market to crash. The costs of the Vietnam War, a devaluation of the U.S. dollar, supply-side inflation and the oil embargo caused the Dow-Jones Index to decline 45 percent during 1973–74.[24]

Amid all of this doom and horror, the Chicago Air and Water Show remained a part of the Lakefront Festival for the duration. Sheathed in polyester, we kept going. Even the show performers adjusted.

Both the Blue Angels and the Thunderbirds were flying the kerosene-gulping smudgepot F-4 Phantom II interceptors, and in the spirit of political and social correctness, they both downsized their rides. In December 1974, the Blue Angels shifted over to the A-4F Skyhawk II. During that same year, the USAF Thunderbirds parked their F-4s for the T-38 Talon, a training plane based on the F-5E, a small export fighter that saw extensive use as an "aggressor" aircraft in combat training with such organizations as the Sixty-fourth Aggressor Squadron and Sixty-fifth Aggressor Squadron at Nellis Air Force Base in Nevada. Five Talons used as much fuel as one F-4 Phantom II.[25] Even with that savings, the Thunderbirds only flew six shows in 1973.

Bigger and Better

A Fat Albert support plane with the Blue Angels' A4F Skyhawk II small fighters for the gas-rationing era of the mid-1970s. *Courtesy Naval Aviation Museum, Pensacola, FL.*

On August 11, 1973, the Thunderbirds shared the air space above Lake Shore Park with an assembly of antique aircraft. Everything from a DC-3 to a post–World War I British Tigermoth biplane and a flying semi-replica of the 1903 Wright Brothers Flyer, complete with a period-costumed pilot and terrified passenger, cruised past the spectators. If those displays did not satisfy the need for aerial thrills, more than 380 purebred homing pigeons were released next to the reviewing stand. The excitable birds, suddenly flung free above the gaping masses, proceeded to strafe the bleachers. Applause turned to strangled cries as the "white rain" pelted down. One splattered woman cried out, "They got me!" A sympathetic Park District employee handed her a cigar as a consolation prize.[26]

The pigeons seemed to set the theme for the 1973 Lakefront Festival, continuing to the Big Parade down State Street led by King Neptune. Following the toot, whistle, plunk and boom of the marching bands, trundling floats and ragged lines of politicians came a sight that made everyone smile. Rank on rank of Belgian draft horses—seven feet tall at the withers with hoofs the size of pie plates—tramped along in polished harness. The forty horses hauled an ornate band wagon belonging to the Schlitz Brewery. To the relief of all the other marching organizations, the clopping, rumbling entourage brought up the rear of the parade as the *whoppeta-boom-bam* of

Homage was paid to the Wright brothers and early aviation during antique airplane flybys. *Courtesy Chicago Park District.*

the bands caused many nervous reactions among the herd. Once again, the Chicago Streets and Sanitation Department formed a following phalanx of motorized street sweepers, which were cheered heartily by the crowd.[27]

The 1973 show was virtually all air, as the water events were shut down because Lake Michigan was high and lapped at the feet of the front bleachers. The navy offered some patrol boats for inspection, and the traditional Venetian Night parade went off on schedule.

While motorists with even-numbered license plates could buy gasoline on even-numbered days and vice versa for odd numbers to spread out available fuel supplies, 1974 limped toward August and great expectations. High water in Lake Michigan once again scuttled speedboats and lifeguard rowing races, but Al Benedict and his staff went for every aerobatic entertainment they could squeeze into the three-hour format. Besides the Thunderbirds and the Golden Knights, the U.S. Army Silver Eagles helicopter team hovered onto the scene with its seven OH-6A Cayuse aircraft.

Between 1972 and 1976, the Silver Eagles performed in more than 220 air shows. As with the Thunderbirds, the Eagles' routines were strictly tactical maneuvers required of all army helicopter pilots. The Eagles used proximity and heart-stopping choreography to show what was possible with the small scout choppers. They flew in a six-plane "wedge," their tight formation regulated by the diameter of their rotor blade arc. Their sound was not the *wup-wup-wup* of the big "Hueys" used as workhorses in Vietnam but rather a collective snarl.

The Silver Eagles flew seven aircraft during each demonstration: lead, left wing, right wing, slot, lead solo, opposing solo and Bozo the Clown. Bozo wore the face of a clown on the fuselage and performed antics to entertain the audience, while the other aircraft were positioning for the next maneuver. Speeds and altitudes of precision maneuvers ranged from 0 miles per hour at ground level to 140 miles per hour at one thousand feet. The most unique thing about the performance was that there was at least one helicopter performing in front of the crowd at all times during the thirty-five-minute presentation.

Another team flew into the mix in 1974, a civilian aerobatic team named the Red Devils flying the latest Pitts Special clipped-wing biplane. Composed of pilots Charlie Hillard, Tom Poberezny and Gene Soucy, the team flew as a group from 1973 to 1978. Gene Soucy was an "air show brat" whose dad, Paul, was a commercial pilot and owned two Pitts Special aircraft, while his mother, Pegge, soloed on her sixteenth birthday and regularly bundled him off to air shows. His dad let him taxi the Pitts from the hangar to the line to get a feel for the plane. After years of flying individually, he and Charlie Hillard became members of the U.S. Aerobatic Team in international competitions. Eventually, they flew with Tom in a couple of shows and formed the Red Devils to pay their way.

The Pitts Special biplane is synonymous with aerobatics. It was designed by Curtis Pitts, a self-taught engineer who had been an airplane inspector during World War II. Pitts worked with his friend Phil Quigley to create the original S-1. This stubby, open-strut biplane had little to recommend it to the FAA inspectors, who failed to award the plane an airworthiness certificate. On his own, Pitts surreptitiously flew the biplane from a field, but the inspectors hid in some trees to watch. Its performance won the certificate. The Pitts S and SS series revolutionized aerobatics, making maneuvers available to pilots that were never thought possible. By increasing its horsepower from the original 55 to over 180 in the "Super Stinker" version, even more aggressive possibilities emerged. Today, the Pitts is still the benchmark of precision aerobatic aviation.[28] In 1974, the Red Devils' show stunned the crowd.

The U.S. Marine Corps brought its latest combat aircraft, which was unique compared to all of the other aircraft in the show. The British Harrier vertical takeoff and landing aircraft—"jump-jet"—was an instant crowd pleaser. Though it was subsonic, the plane's ability to take off straight up, transition into level flight and hurtle across the lakeshore to return and hover in place like a helicopter drew a burst of cheers. The Harrier allowed the British to create troop support carriers with shorter, "ski-jump" decks, and it gave them a troop support aircraft that could land and take off virtually anywhere in the combat theatre. The plane proved its value in the Falkland Islands campaign against the Argentine army. U.S. Marine Corps aviation has a similar troop support mission; it adopted the plane with considerable success.

The Great Lakes Navy Band sat out the 1974 show, replaced by the musical styling of Frankie Masters and his orchestra. Jerry G. Bishop, the original Svengoolie who hosted Chicago's ghoulish horror movie showcase, Screaming Yellow Theatre, from 1970 to 1973, served as emcee. He shared the chore with news anchorperson and professional celebrity Linda Alvarez, with special guests Jaye P. Morgan and Tommy Bartlett of water-ski show fame.

The Seventeenth Annual Chicago Air and Water Show in 1975 once again sent the U.S. Navy Blue Angels off from Glenview Naval Air Station. The U.S. Army Golden Knights parachute team climbed into its blue and gold trimmed C-47 at Meigs Field for its ride over Lake Shore Park, the plummet and convolutions of choreography ending in wet splashdown. The jumpers went from the lifeguard rowboats to shore and then to the park field house, where they draped their jumpsuits and parachutes from the basketball hoops in the gym and dried them out with rented blow-dryers. For the performers, there was a comforting familiarity to the ritual—soggy landing and all.[29] For the audience, the same comforting expectations were fulfilled, but with a taste of something new added each time.

During the 1975 show, Walt Pierce beat up the air in front of the Lake Shore Park bleachers, piloting his 450 Stearman, "Old Smokey" biplane painted red, white and blue with a checkered tail. Walt got bit by the flying bug when, as a young boy, he passed a fenced-in collection of beat-up BT-13 Vultee Valiant training planes in New Mexico. Nicknamed the "Vibrator" because of its predilection to heavy vibration every time it came near stalling speed, all of these low-wing monoplanes had their 450-horsepower engines sliced off the front to be attached to Stearman biplanes. Pierce didn't mind. He claimed that he sat in those cockpits and put in "10,000 hours of BT-13 time and never took one off the ground."

Often, the lake winds scattered the parachutists diving into the lake, and the lifeguard boats had to scramble to retrieve them. *Courtesy Chicago Park District.*

At age sixteen, Walt became a flag boy, marking fields for crop dusters' passes with a colored flag. Soon, he was flying the pesticide-loaded Stearman biplanes to the remote dirt airstrips where the duster pilots took over. After a tour in the U.S. Air Force as a mechanic, he got his pilot's license and began flying a 1929 Great Lakes Sport Trainer two-seat biplane. Eventually, he began working for Frank Price, a legendary aerobatic pilot who doubled for

Above: Police lifeboats and park district lifeguard boats retrieved Golden Knights parachutists from the lake in the 1960s and '70s. *Courtesy Chicago Park District.*

Below: No one doubts a trace of whimsy in the park district planner's agenda, as shown here in the 1970s. *Courtesy Chicago Park District.*

the actor who played Ernst Kessler in the movie *The Great Waldo Pepper*. By 1971, Walt assembled his own mini air show, with Sandi Pierce as his wing walker, and took it on the road. Sandi also flew a Great Lakes Sport Trainer as an aerial performer.

By 1976, after sixteen weekend performances, the Air and Water Show had a self-perpetuating life of its own, but that bicentennial year would see some conclusions and foretell a change of direction. Like the rest of the nation, with the Vietnam nightmare in the past, Chicago was alight with patriotic fervor. Mayor Richard J. Daley had just been reelected to an unprecedented sixth four-year term by a crushing landslide, which pushed the police and demonstrator riots of the 1968 Democratic Convention debacle even further behind him. American flags flew everywhere, and the largest fireworks display in Chicago history was planned for the gala lakefront July Fourth celebration.

The usual capacity crowd filled the center stage area at Lake Shore Park and spilled over to the north and south. Navy Pier had rehabbed its grand ballroom for bicentennial events after five years of disuse. An increasing air show audience presence on Navy Pier was causing the FAA some concern since it was against the air show rules to have a demonstration plane's nose pointed at the audience. The usual suspects played out their skills with the usual success, and the Blue Angels entertained everyone, as did the ubiquitous Golden Knights.

With the same precision as exhibited at the last show, the Silver Eagles helicopter demonstration team appeared in formation trailing white smoke. This was the team's fourth year on the show circuit, and it had learned it was also the last. The U.S. Army was disbanding the unit, but the Eagles played out their 1976 schedule anyway with their usual panache to the end.

Another precision flying act that would not return swooped down onto the stage, and Ed Mahler began tossing around his biplane coupled to a Parsons-Jocelyn 285-horsepower engine. Mahler had won fame with the U.S. Aerobatic Team. The tall, lanky pilot was in demand across the country, and his performance brought cheers from the more than 300,000 spectators. Mahler was sponsored by Mennen Aftershave Lotion, and as he concluded his act, he made one last pass across the audience and released a smoke trail. As the smoke wafted by the lakeshore bleachers, audience members sniffed the signature scent of Mennen Aftershave. Commercially sponsored events had arrived at the Air and Water Show.

The following year, at West Hampton, New York, Mahler flew at the Suffolk County Airport show on September 24. After wringing his biplane out in an aerobatic display, he landed to make a repair on one of the struts that supported his tail section. He remarked to a helper on the flight line that the repair was "no big deal." His next job was to fly inverted across the airport and slice a ribbon tied between two poles thirty feet apart with his tail. This was standard aerobatic fare, and he zoomed off to get the job done. In a few moments, he returned, flipped on his back and headed for the poles and ribbon. As he approached, his tail began to wobble—and then it tore away from the fuselage. The biplane arced straight down for three hundred feet into the concrete and exploded.

Ed Mahler was forty-three, a twenty-year veteran of the air show circuit, and he left behind a wife and ten-year-old daughter.[30]

Ed Mahler's death was tragic, but it was a distant event in time and space from the Chicago shore. Another death had a more direct impact on the show and the lakefront celebrations. Enjoying great popularity in his twenty-first year as Chicago's undisputed "Boss," Mayor Richard Daley suffered a massive coronary while visiting his doctor and died on December 20. It was as if all the breeze had gone out of the Windy City's sails. For all his political maneuvering, rubber-stamp city council and rule-by-caveat philosophy, Daley was quietly loved and/or respected by the people he governed. Like the Air and Water Show, he had become a tradition, a known commodity, and always had something new to offer or, in his case, demand. Christmas was coming, but throughout the city the faithful lit candles in memory of the Boss they had known since 1955.

As the show moved along from year to year and continued on as a regular summer event, the trick was how to come up with something new. Up until about the tenth year, the only money that flowed into the Lake Shore Park budget came from donations. Volunteers offered the manpower to fill the dozens of critical jobs. Publicity was dependent on the local *Chicago Tribune*, *Daily News*, *Herald American* and *Sun Times*, as well as the *Near North News* run by Arnie Matanky. But eventually the logistics and performance fees got just too big, and the show's success had also grown, along with the crowds overflowing Lake Shore Park to the north and south. Matanky eventually became the public-relations mouthpiece for the Chicago Park District.

Finally, some phone calls were made, meetings were held and the event officially became the Chicago Park District Air and Water Show. It continued, however, to keep Al Benedict, its founder, as the show's director.

CHAPTER 5

THE SHOW ENDURES

NEW HANDS AT THE HELM

With the death of Richard J. Daley in 1976, the mayor's job passed into the hands of Michael A. Bilandic. In 1977, Bilandic promised the "greatest" festival to put his own stamp on the collection of summer events. Since he was busy trying to collect the reins of all the city council horses that drove the Chicago machine, his stamp was limited to ordering a batch of searchlights and pointing them up. This Hollywood-premier effect became the "Temple of Light" in the press releases from the office of Joe Balasa, the new director of the mayor's special events. Colonel Jack Reilly had no reason to remain in Chicago with his friend and liege lord gone, so he retired to Fort Lauderdale, Florida, where he died of a heart attack in July 1988 at age eighty-nine.[31]

On Saturday, August 13, the big King Neptune Day Parade stepped off with Mayor Bilandic and Miss Snow Zecevic, the Lake Front Festival queen. Unfortunately, the fire department's fireboat, the *Victor Schlaeger*, was positioned to loose arches of colored water high above the State Street Bridge as the mayoral/Neptune party crossed. Fortunately for King Neptune, he reached the south bank to the cheers of his subjects just before a brisk lakeside wind caught the tons of water jetting from the fireboat's water cannon. Unfortunately, the mayor, in his best blue yachting blazer, vanished under the cascade of red, white and blue semi-toxic river water. Miss Zecevic wore a bathing suit and only suffered her puffy hairdo being plastered to her head and her eyeliner running down her cheeks. The mayor and the queen gamely sloshed on down State Street looking like drowning victims.

In the 1970s, the beauty queens were still part of the attraction of the Lake Shore Park Show. *Courtesy Chicago Park District.*

The Air and Water Show was once again incorporated into the Lakefront Festival as the Blue Angels roared overhead and the Golden Knights plopped into the lake, followed by the Harrier Jump Jet hovering above the waves.

The Hawker-Siddeley Vulcan bomber of the Royal Air Force returned and was scheduled to star in the 1978 Air and Water Show. That year, the name of the overall two weeks of hoopla was changed to ChicagoFest. Though the Lakefront Festival limped on, planners announced that the name would vanish in a year or two and the Gold Coast Art Fair, polka contests, marathon swim races, aerial thrill show at Daley Plaza and Portage Park Water Polo Championships would become ChicagoFest events.

On August 12, rehearsal day for the Air and Water Show, the Vulcan bomber with four of its crew took off from Glenview Naval Air Station for a quick run over the lake. Shortly after takeoff, the four-engine, delta-wing jet lost power, and fuel was seen to vent as the plane began a turn to head back to the airfield. Gliding silently above blocks of homes and schools, the plane banked away from its rapidly descending glide path and came down across the Chicago and Northwestern Railroad tracks into a landfill, skidded about

The longest-lasting segment was the air-sea rescue by various government units; shown is a Chicago Fire Department demonstration. *Courtesy Chicago Park District.*

two hundred yards, broke in half and detonated in a huge fireball. All four crew members were killed, and the pilot was deemed a hero for steering the crippled craft away from occupied houses.

The show went on as scheduled, and the USAF Thunderbirds flew their usual routine. Otherwise, the town was alight with fireworks displays, the traditional Bud Billiken Parade on the South Side, a Japanese Ginza Festival, a sand sculpture contest, polka dances and the largest square dance in the country. One additional added event was a Hare and Hound Race by balloonists, who took off from Grant Park to circle back after a few hours and land as close to the "Hare" balloon as possible.

On August 19, the balloon race competitors departed on time from Grant Park. The Hare balloon was all black and decorated with skull and crossbones. No sooner was it aloft than those pesky winds that had dogged the aviators who had used Grant Park as their "aerodrome" during the 1911 Aviation Meet struck again. One by one, the hapless balloonists were swept out over vast Lake Michigan. As spectators munched sandwiches and waited…and waited…the balloons became specks and then vanished altogether. Everybody went home. The Hare and Hound Race ended with competitors scattered all around fields and woods near Hobart, Indiana.

The summer extravaganza was Mayor Bilandic's last hurrah. With winter clamping down, Chicago was buried under a huge, lingering snowfall. Snowplows fell behind the accumulation; salt was in short supply. Aldermen were deluged with complaints. The mayoral campaign of 1979 saw Jane Byrne sweeping into the fifth-floor office by showing voters photos of their clogged streets.

A hue and cry went up over Mayor Byrne's contention that the 1978 ChicagoFest had lost $400,000, and she threatened to scuttle the 1979 events. However, House Majority Leader Michael Madigan rammed a million-dollar grant to support the Fest through the General Assembly in Springfield. He sucked it out of downstate agriculture funds, leaving state and county fair folks feeling pillaged and burned. Madigan explained that this move granted Chicago equal consideration for financing a Cook County fair.

That year, some up-front promotion heralded the Air and Water Show, which was scheduled for late July for the first time. To announce the coming show, ten of the Golden Knights stepped out of their airplane at twelve thousand feet to free-fall for eight thousand feet in a wedge formation and then open their chutes to land in a small target zone on Meigs Field. The show in 1979 was a navy and air force recruiter's delight, as the Blue Angels flew led by a Chicagoan, Lieutenant Commander Bill Newman, with pilot Jack Ekt of Hinsdale flying in the diamond. Military performers also included—besides the Golden Knights—the 126th Air Refueling Squadron of the Illinois National Guard, the RAF Vulcan bomber and the world's largest airplane, the C5-A Galaxy.

Mayor Jane Byrne talks with the Golden Knights at the Air and Water Show during her term. *Courtesy Chicago Park District.*

Often referred to as FRED—"F***ing Ridiculous Economic/ Environmental Disaster"—by its crews because of its maintenance issues (requiring sixteen hours of maintenance for each flight hour, based on 1996 data) and its consumption of fuel, the 1970 aircraft is one of the largest planes in the world. It is a high-wing cargo transporter with a high T-tail and is powered by four GE TF39 turbofan jet engines. Its cargo compartment—open at both ends of the plane—is about one foot longer than the Wright brothers' flight at Kitty Hawk in 1903.[32] Every statistic concerning the C5-A is a superlative. Its swept-wing appearance, looming above the crowd, always draws headshakes and hushed silence.

The Canadian Reds pilots, Bill Cowan and Rod Ellis, provided the propeller-driven aerial excitement for the 1979 program. This pair of pilots looping, diving and smoking up the air in their Pitts S2A biplanes to the cheers of the crowd originally formed the Carlings Red Cap team. Anyone who has lived near the Canadian border has had the opportunity to down a few bottles of Carlings Red Cap Ale. Skil Tools bought the sponsorship of the Red Caps and made them the Canadian Reds. Subsequently, Bausch & Lomb picked up the tab, and the two Pitts Special stunt planes became the Ray Ban Golds, named after a new line of sunglasses.[33]

The point of this commercial litany is the continued inroads sponsored entertainment was making in the air show circuit. These acts, with the airplanes splattered with logo decals and bright paint jobs, were following the same path as Indianapolis racers and NASCAR stock cars—zooming billboards in front of captive audiences. This trend, whether extolling the virtues of Skil Tools, the fragrance of Mennen Aftershave Lotion or the sex appeal of Ray Ban gold-rimmed sunglasses, took some of the financial burden off the shoulders of air show fundraisers and municipal budgets. Apparently, the sponsors saw an impact on their bottom line because the air show has endured long after other "pure" specialty sports have faded away.

All that the air show organizer had to provide was a large enough head count to justify the expenses incurred by splashing the sponsor's brand across the skies. Chicago program organizers, despite the basic sameness of each scheduled performance, managed to infuse enough new elements each time to guarantee not just a minimum fixed number of spectators but also a growing number of enthusiasts. The military had already pioneered the concept of glamorous demonstration teams to promote recruiting. Thanks to Al Benedict, the Chicago Park District had hit on the correct Chicago Air and Water Show formula. The 1979 show entertained an estimated 500,000 Chicagoans and tourists.

One other local touch remained in the expanded schedule of events. As in 1959, the original audience for the spectacle was the kids in the Park District Day Camp program. They were not forgotten twenty years later. Acres of day campers paraded from downtown Chicago to Lake Shore Park, where they had ringside seats to a special rehearsal of the weekend demonstrations and excitement furnished by the Blue Angels, the Coast Guard helicopters and other acts. Who knew that in twenty years these kids would bring their kids to the same Air and Water Show, perpetuating the tradition?

As the calendar rolled over into the 1980s, the first show of the new decade started out breaking with the past format. For the first time, both the

Opposite, top: The Coast Guard Air Rescue was the earliest air feature and continued from 1959 to the present. *Courtesy Chicago Park District.*

Opposite, bottom: Al Benedict in line with the USAF Thunderbirds flight demonstration team in 1982. He was the driving force behind the show. *Courtesy Chicago Park District.*

Blue Angels and the USAF Thunderbirds performed over Lake Shore Park. Sharing the sky with the American teams were the Canadian Reds in their Pitts Special biplanes. Another really exciting aerobatic team to perform was the French Connection. Daniel Heligoin and his wife, Montaine Mallet, were international champion aerobatic stars and had flown together in their matching CAP10s for over twenty-five years. They billed themselves as a husband-and-wife aerial ballet and flew their act to prerecorded, self-narrated poetry and custom-composed music. Their signature move was a canopy-to-canopy, 360-degree circle, with only inches between cockpits, ending with a rollout.

Avions Mudry of France, who sponsored the pair, produced the CAP-10B ("Constructions Aéronautiques Parisiennes") bubble-cockpit, low-wing monoplane with fixed landing gear that they flew in shows. Developed by Auguste Mudry from the Piel Super Emeraude, the wood aircraft featured side-by-side seating and dual controls. Its engine was a Lycoming AEIO-360 fuel-injected plant that was still fully lubricated in inverted flight. The plane entered production in 1971.[34]

Daniel and Montaine were awarded the Bill Barber Award for Showmanship in 1987 and served on the award's selection committee. They were also past recipients of the Art Scholl Memorial Showmanship Award. Both were known in the aerobatic community as highly skilled aviators, always willing to share their expertise—and their love—of flying.

On May 27, 2000, they were making a promotional video over their home field in Flagler, Florida, when they entered a third hammerhead stall. As they rotated 180 degrees out of their upward climb, the plane's low-wing design caused Daniel to lose sight of Montaine's plane as they started to come together in a belly-to-belly formation before rolling out. In the nose-down position, at about seven hundred feet from the ground, their wings sheared together, ripping off control surfaces. Out of control, the two pilots flew straight into the ground, ending their long partnership in a final pas de deux.[35]

As Chicago entered the decade of the Me Generation, the Twenty-third Annual Chicago Park District Air and Water Show in 1981 endured despite low cloud cover on Saturday and Sunday performances. The French Connection returned, and the Canadian Snowbirds upheld the military precision flight contingent.

Officially, the 431st Air Demonstration Squadron, the Snowbirds are a nine-pilot team flying CT-114 Tutor two-place jets ordered by the RCAF in 1961. These subsonic ground-attack and training aircraft—known

Comedian Bill Murray fastened to a U.S. Army Golden Knight parachutist as the team plummets toward North Avenue Beach in 2008 to celebrate the fiftieth presentation of the Air and Water Show. *Courtesy Mayor's Office of Special Events.*

The Blue Angels in diamond formation over North Avenue Beach in 2008. *Courtesy Mayor's Office of Special Events.*

Gary Jet Center with its apron filled with parked F-16 Falcons just flown in by the USAF Thunderbirds. *Courtesy Gerry Souter.*

A fireboat sends water in arcs from its water cannon off North Avenue Beach during the water part of the 2009 show. *Courtesy Gerry Souter.*

Members of the Aeroshell aerobatic team photographed from the rear cockpit in 2009 before they launched into one of their routines. *Courtesy Janet Souter.*

Opposite, top: On shore during the 2008 celebration of the fiftieth presentation of the Chicago Air and Water Show, the Jesse White tumblers entertain the North Avenue Beach crowds with one of their spectacular routines. *Courtesy Mayor's Office of Special Events.*

Opposite, bottom: Sean Tucker blazes past the Chicago skyline behind North Avenue Beach in his red Oracle Pitts Special Challenger biplane. *Courtesy Gerry Souter.*

Above: Air and Water Show crowds spread from rooftops to Oak Street Beach in 2004. *Courtesy Mayor's Office of Special Events.*

Right: Chicago World's Fair attendees in 1893 could rise one thousand feet above the White City in this tethered gas-filled balloon for a view that reached to the distant suburbs. *Courtesy Library of Congress.*

The U.S. postage stamp issued to commemorate the Graf Zeppelin's visit to the Chicago Century of Progress Fair in 1933. *Courtesy Dan Grossman, http://www.airships.net.*

The 1911 Chicago International Aviation Meet was held on the lakefront in Grant Park. American and European pilots competed for records and prize money over nine days in front of millions of spectators. *Courtesy Library of Congress.*

Opposite: A Chicago Air and Water Show poster, 2003. *Courtesy Gavin Fine Art & Design.*

© 2003 GAVIN FINE ART & DESIGN   www.gavinarts.com

CHICAGO

AIR & WATER SHOW

CENTENNIAL OF FLIGHT

City of Chicago
Richard M. Daley, Mayor

FEATURING THE

USAF THUNDERBIRDS
AUGUST 16-17, 2003

SATURDAY & SUNDAY 9:00am - 4:00pm

ON CHICAGO'S LAKEFRONT AT NORTH AVENUE BEACH

PRESENTED BY

Shell *and the* City of Chicago

FOR MORE INFORMATION

Hotline: 312-744-3370   TTY: 312-744-2964

www.cityofchicago.org/SpecialEvents/

Two Blue Angels "walk" their fighters on their tails across part of the yacht fleet in Lake Michigan—a stunning demonstration of flight control. *Courtesy Mayor's Office of Special Events.*

affectionately as "Toot"—were designed and built by Canadair. They are modified for aerobatics by the addition of a smoke generator and a fine-tuned engine for low-slow flying. Their flight program starts with an impressive nine-plane flyby, keeping very tight formation, and evolves into nine-plane group maneuvers—turns, slow rolls and climbs—before breaking up into solo head-ons and starbursts if altitude situations permit. Their planes sport a red and white paint scheme with white wings painted over the red underbellies.

The military star of the 1981 show, however, was the formerly top-secret SR-71 Blackbird. The CIA "spook" reconnaissance aircraft is capable of speeds three times that of sound. This ultra high altitude spy plane operated beyond any air-to-ground missile defense system, and its flights were highly classified. Powered by two Pratt & Whitney J-59 Axial-flow turbojets with afterburners, each producing 32,500 pounds of thrust, the big jet had a ceiling of over eighty-five thousand feet and an un-refueled range of two thousand miles. Even after it retired and became an air show highlight, it was still the fastest plane in the world to take off under its own power. Its rumbling 1981 flyby of the Chicago lakefront gave Chicagoans a glimpse of the pinnacle of American air power.

Low cloud cover almost canceled the wing-walking act of Bob and Pat Wagner, who had been entertaining crowds for more than thirty years. The clouds broke enough for Pat to stand atop the WACO (pronounced "Wahco") biplane while her husband looped and rolled it above the lake.

The grand week of festivities called the Lakefront Festival had largely disappeared when Jane Byrne became mayor. She added to what had become known as ChicagoFest, including a new eating event called Taste of Chicago with over fifty food stands from Chicago restaurants selling samples from their menus along Michigan Avenue from Wacker Drive to Ohio Street on July 4. As part of the Summertime Chicago events, a music festival and minority-owned restaurant stands were set up on Navy Pier from August 1 through August 17. Traditional Venetian Night was scheduled for August 22.

By 1981, the Taste of Chicago had been moved to Grant Park, running from July 3 to July 5. The number of food and beverage vendors increased from fifty to eighty, with free admission. The entire lakefront became a collection of entertainment venues that included the Air and Water Show on July 25 and 26 amid food, music, boat parades and other participation events. Main stage entertainers for ChicagoFest included: Bobby Vinton, Crystal Gayle, John Prine, Steve Goodman, Aretha Franklin, the Four

The "Big Buff" B-52 bomber, built in 1952, was still flying missions in 2009. No plane matches its payload and flight-endurance time. *Courtesy Mayor's Office of Special Events.*

Tops, Air Supply, the Rossington Collins Band, the Dick Clark Rock and Roll Show, Mickey Gilley, Johnny Lee, the Urban Cowboy Band and Hank Williams Jr.

While all of the Summertime Chicago events were in play, only the Air and Water Show remained a solid fixture in Chicago's summer lakefront entertainment. It was reassuring to know that it was there, anchoring the North Shore.

Weather for show number twenty-four was hot, with a cloudless, scalding blue sky filled with soaring aircraft, as the water seethed with boats and water events. A P3 Aurora antisubmarine patrol plane picked its way along the shoreline. This reconnaissance aircraft was originally the U.S. Orion P3C created from the basic airframe of the Electra passenger liner. It was powered by four Allison T56-14 turboprops. Eighteen airframes were modified for Canadian service and called the Aurora CP-140. Dwarfing the Aurora was the jumbo mass of a B-52 bomber—still a frontline USAF weapon destined to play a role in the Gulf War even though it was built in the early 1950s. But the shadow that put the big "Big Buf" in the shade came from an overflight of a C-5A Galaxy making an encore appearance as the world's largest airplane.

An F-15 Strike Eagle howls above the spectators during a high-speed pass. *Courtesy Mayor's Office of Special Events.*

The McDonnell-Douglas F-15 Eagle suddenly bellowed above the shoreline spectators, ripping along just below the speed of sound and then climbing like an arrow into the high blue. The Eagle was an "air superiority" fighter, replacing the F4 Phantom II in 1968. Its twin tail and twin jets were distinctive, as was its compact frame. Countering the huge Soviet Foxbat super-fighter, the F-15 Eagle hummed along at Mach 2.5 and carried Sidewinder missiles and a Vulcan M61 rotary cannon. Wringing out the thoroughbred required a hot hand and a good G-suit to counter the stresses that went with flying "by wire" in maneuvers dictated by a rapidly calculating computer. The development of the F-15, which was deemed a "heavyweight" by the USAF, led to the eventual production of the F-16 Fighting Falcon as the "lightweight" capability equivalent.[36]

Whatever the future held for the F-15 Eagle, boaters bobbing in the lake just outside the break wall had to open their mouths and stuff plugs in their ears when the shrieking fighter went vertical, pushed by its twin afterburners. They were thankful that the FAA frowned on sudden bursts of supersonic speed at air shows.

If the 1982 show was a blazing success, the twenty-fifth anniversary of the Air and Water Show in 1983 was off the charts. Any airplane buff casually glancing at the pre-show pamphlet put out by the Chicago Park District would have had to take a pill and sit down. The lineup included:

USAF Thunderbirds
Canadian Snowbirds
C-5A Galaxy transport
126th Air Refueling Squadron, Illinois National Guard
Chicago Fire Department Helicopter and Marine Unit
Chicago Police Department Marine Unit
The RAF Vulcan Bomber
Pair o' Sixes SNJ Aerobatic Team
Ray Ban Gold Squadron with three Pitts Special biplanes
C-130 Hercules, 928th Tactical Air Group, USAF Reserve
U.S. Coast Guard Air-Sea Rescue Unit
A nine-plane demonstration unit from the Italian air force to mark the fiftieth
    anniversary of Balbo's flight and arrival at Chicago
A paddleboat named *Betsy-Anne*

There would be a lot of sore necks in Chicago before the end of Sunday. The Italian contingent—Frecce Tricolori—was on hand to take part in the celebration planned by the Museum of Science and Industry commemorating the fiftieth anniversary of Italo Balbo's flight to Chicago and the 1933 Century of Progress. His fleet of twenty-four seaplanes, which arrived on Chicago's lakefront en masse during their around-the-world flight to promote Fascism, had stirred much controversy. This time, however, the flock of ten Aermacchi MB-33 jet fighters represented just an Italian long-distance flight pioneer, who, it turned out later, was no friend of dictator Benito Mussolini. The Chicago newspapers opened the old wounds, as did their op-ed pages, with prominent Chicago Italian-Americans denouncing the celebration. The fact that we had a Balbo Drive and a Balbo monument erected on the lakefront grass added to the affront. Besides the planes, one hundred cadets and five officers of the Italian navy's air force were also attending the July 15–17 ceremonies.[37]

Police estimated that over 725,000 ventured out into the ninety-degree steamy summer weather. Sunday brought some rain, but crowds returned after the brief storm just as the Thunderbirds—the wrap-up act—howled across the lakefront at 5:00 p.m. in their new F-16 Fighting Falcon jets.[38]

The Show Endures

Sadly, 1983 sang the swan song for Jane Byrne's brief stay as mayor. After breaking the gender glass ceiling, Chicago voters decided to experiment with racial diversity and elected African American Harold Washington to reign over city hall. The white majority of aldermen at city hall threw up their hands and announced the end of the world, but, surprisingly, the city proved to be an adaptable community.

At the Twenty-sixth Air and Water Show in July 1984, the Golden Knights once again floated down toward 500,000 spectators packed in and around Lake Shore Park. The Blue Angels blasted through their routines, and the U.S. Coast Guard plucked "victims" from the lake with red and white helicopters. Even Al Benedict, the founder and still the director of the program, shook his head at the monster he had created.

"The first show was a local water show that lasted forty minutes," he said. "I never would have thought that such a little show would become something like this. There's people watching this for miles. It's incredible."

Benedict remembered a lot of sleepless nights and last-minute panics over the years. He also remembered the funny bits, the crowd-pleasers created by his staff:

> *One time, before their show, the Golden Knights pilots were lined up on Meigs Field to meet me, the show director. It was a pretty solemn moment, the big cheese meeting these parachutists all standing at attention. The limousine rolls up to the presentation area. The driver jumps out and swings open the rear door—and out scrambles Moses, the Lincoln Park Zoo chimpanzee. Everyone went nuts.*

His staff assistant Rudy Malnati, who now virtually runs the current show, remembers the parking problems that plagued the Lake Shore Park and Outer Drive area. The police were forever shooing drivers off the shoulder of the drive to move along. Parking in Streeterville was packed bumper to bumper, as were the Armory and Lake Shore Park field. Cops wrote a lot of tickets.

"One day," Malnati recalled,

> *a voice comes booming over the public address speakers as the show is going on, "Ladies and Gentlemen, would the driver of a late model, red..." And he describes the car and plate number. "Please remove your vehicle from its illegal parking space." A little later, he reads the announcement again and finally reads it a third time, adding "This is your final warning." Then, from behind*

the crowd comes this engine rumble and wup-wup-wup *of propeller blades. A big Sikorski crane helicopter appears and below it, hanging from a wire and hook is this "illegally parked car." The helicopter soars around the audience and out over the lake. Just offshore, the pilot releases the hook, and the car drops into the lake and sinks. Everybody goes nuts. Of course we'd stripped a good-looking junkyard car of its motor and seats and made a cardboard license plate, but everyone bought it as hard-nosed traffic cop justice.*

Of course, you can't do that today, what with the environment people around, but back then we got away with it. What a great gag.

That year, farewells were also said to ChicagoFest, which Jane Byrne had picked up from Mayor Bilandic to scatter baubles of entertainment among the electorate. The festival collective was scuttled. For seven years, Chicagoans had gotten their summer fun fix courtesy of Festivals, Inc. The Milwaukee-based consulting firm had received $1 million a year—that was significant money in 1984—to create and supply entertainment venues. Money was no object. Frank Sinatra claimed $200,000 for a fifty-five-minute performance, while Liza Minnelli strode off the stage at the Chicago Theatre after two performances with a $300,000 paycheck. If the festival had sold every seat in the house, it stood to make $10,000 or $20,000. An oversight committee had been appointed by Byrne to screen the restaurants for Taste of Chicago on Navy Pier, but clout-wielding aldermen brought in restaurants for favors and kickbacks that nobody had screened. Politics and bloated budgets sank the city's summer fun.

Except, of course, for the Air and Water Show, which came off without a hitch for the twenty-sixth time.

Bob Bishop had his hands full of one big hitch in 1985 as his Coors Silver Bullet jet plane whistled down the lakeshore. The control stick jumped in his hands, the airframe vibrated and his teeth chattered as the Windy City put on a show of steamy hot westerly breezes that boiled in front of his nose and buffeted all over his control services. He wrestled with a jet aircraft only twelve feet long with a seventeen-foot wingspan and weighing about 432 pounds. It had been built from a kit requiring 350 hours of labor.[39] Bishop's voice was patched into the public address system, and it sounded like he was flying inside a blender.

"This wind…makes the b-b-b-bumps even b-b-bumpier," he informed the crowd. "Oh boy, is it ever…b-b-bumpy!"

Unable to throw the petit Microjet—which had made its mark in a recent James Bond film, *Octopussy*, flying through a hangar pursued by a missile—into its aerobatic routine because of the sixty-mile-per-hour winds, he made a three-hundred-mile-per-hour pass…*Fizzzoooot!*…and was gone. The show announcer immediately reassured the audience that the Silver Bullet would return on Sunday for the next show. Down at water level, thirty-five-mile-per-hour winds tossed the Chicago All-Stars water-skiers about, ending many precise routines in a wet tangle. Three-year-old Kelly Lagore of Chicago was blown onto her backside into the three inches of water that lapped up the toward the bleacher seats. Amidst all the acts that were not heavy enough to bowl their way through the muggy winds—such as the F-15 Eagle and C-130 transports—the Golden Knights parachute team timed its jump perfectly. The Knights wafted down to arrive at center stage, aiming at red "target" buoys bobbing in the waves.[40]

The big news of the 1985 Air and Water Show was the immense tangle of humanity and automobiles that clogged Lake Shore Drive and effectively imprisoned the residents of Streeterville for the duration of the weekend. In addition to the press of bodies crammed onto the water's edge, high-rise apartments became party centers, and tenants brought in friends and relatives sated with liberal quantities of food and booze to watch the show from open windows and behind picture-window expanses of hermetically sealed glass.

"People from nearby high-rises are always calling me," said Al Benedict, "to make sure they have the right dates so they can plan their parties. It's unbelievable that it has grown to this size."[41]

Though the show program had been refined and choreographed into safe entertainments featuring all manner of potentially lethal military hardware and scary civilian aerobatic stunts, the spectators were stretching the seams of their lakefront amphitheatre. For Chicagoans who were not part of the 500,000 to 700,000 spectators, the North Shore, Streeterville and the Gold Coast became one big No-Drive Zone. The other problem was Navy Pier. The late-lamented ChicagoFest had been scheduled to begin after the Air and Water Show due to the Taste of Chicago and other events that drew thousands onto this finger extending out into the lake.

The FAA had cleared pleasure boats from inside the break wall that paralleled the North Shore protecting the lake frontage from heavy wave action. Boaters could gather east of the break wall since it was outside the "box" marked with buoys and fire and police boats that prescribed the "stage" above which the aircraft could fly. This imaginary rectangle also

A signature maneuver of the Blue Angels is their diamond starburst. *Courtesy Mayor's Office of Special Events.*

paralleled the shore and established a line of flight at right angles to the spectators. The jet pilots were given two immutable limits: they could not fly above cloud cover or below one thousand feet, and they could not point the nose of their aircraft at the audience.

Most pilots and precision flight teams handled the altitude restriction by creating "high," "low" and "flat" versions of their show maneuvers. They added or threw out stunts to match the weather conditions. The borders of the box offered other challenges. With the show performed in front of Lake Shore Park, the growing attendance had pushed out to both Oak Street Beach and Navy Pier. This placed Navy Pier parallel to the short leg of the box rectangle and, according to the FAA, in harm's way.

If the 1985 show turned the spotlight on the obvious location problems, the next year's Air and Water Show presentation exacerbated the situation when the sponsoring Park District insisted that the show go on as planned. In 1986, it was estimated that one million spectators would have to be shoehorned into Lake Shore Park and beyond. Ben Bently, spokesman for the Park District, was adamant. "The district plans to hold the show on July 12 and 13. However," he added, "the planes may be asked to fly a little farther offshore."

SOAR, the Streeterville Organization of Active Residents, would have none of it. Noisy meetings brought forth pages of complaints, from litter left on lawns to spectators peeing on hydrangea bushes. "People get obnoxious and do things around the buildings that they shouldn't—really disgusting things," pleaded one resident. Another Streeterville homeowner added, "It's a great city function and people are excited about it year after year and it's tradition. On the other hand, it is damaging to the lawns and the property along the drive."

Park Board president Walter Netsch—part of a new management group—admitted, "The show has become so very popular, it has become an intrusion on the people who live in the Streeterville area. We are now looking for other places to hold the show."[42]

So, with SOAR members grinding their teeth and snapping photos of garbage piles, urinating miscreants, double-parkers and litter-tossers, and the FAA insisting that Navy Pier be removed from the flight danger zone, the 1986 Air and Water Show proceeded for the last, and twenty-sixth, time on its home ground.

The stars of the 1986 show were a considerable departure from the usual suspects. The Patrouille de France, flying in an eight-plane formation and trailing red, white and blue smoke, brought cheers from the crowded shore

Huge crowds at Lake Shore Park, shown here in the late 1970s, eventually became too big for the venue and too annoying for high-rise residents. *Courtesy Chicago Park District.*

as they rushed overhead in their equally red, white and blue Alpha Jets. This plane is a two-seater joint Franco-German product. While the Germans use the Alpha Jet as a secondary role strike fighter, the French prefer its two-seat training capability. The Alpha Jet is a high-wing fighter pushed along by two 1,350-kilogram SNECMA/Turbomeca Lazrac O4-C5 jet engines. Following the European model, the plane is cheap to build and easy to maintain. In the hands of the Patrouille de France pilots, it is an outstanding performer in a limited, but flexible, aerobatic role.[43]

To hold up the USAF end of the program, supplementing the C-5A Galaxy and other frequent performers, was a pair of Raven F-111B fighter-bombers. The sight of a pair of these storied aircraft that worked through early design teething troubles thoroughly entertained aircraft buffs in the audience. The revolutionary planes employed a "swing-wing," which allowed the full wingspan to be deployed for slow maneuvering and subsonic bombing. The wing then swung back toward the fuselage to achieve a swept-wing configuration for supersonic flight. This nuclear-capable, multi-role aircraft was designed as a side-by-side two-seater in a capsule that was ejected with both crewmen in case of emergency bailout. The power plant was a pair of Pratt & Whitney TF-30 turbofan engines each rated at between 18,500 and 25,000 pounds of thrust. The F-111B Raven was both a tactical-strike fighter-bomber and an electronic warfare (EW) aircraft designed to locate and neutralize enemy radar-controlled missile installations. In Vietnam, they were called "Wild Weasels" for their radar-directed, antiaircraft fire suppression role.

The "swing-wing" transition feature was the subject of many problems in the aircraft's early development. Its in-flight deployment caused numerous accidents and groundings of the original designs.[44]

As the big fighter-bombers roared past, spectators cheered, but many residents, now made super-sensitive to the proximity of such speed and raw power, voiced uneasy concerns. The two Ray Ban Gold stunt biplanes zoomed and looped through their routine in front of the steel and glass residence where Beatrice Atschuler lived and watched from her shaded lawn chair.

"It's dangerous to have them here in such a populated area," she said. A friend, Mildred McGurk, seated near her added, "I'd like to see it moved down the lakefront to where there are no apartments. When you're by a window, you think they're coming right in there with you."[45]

Thus ended the Twenty-eighth Annual Air and Water Show. As the hot, tired, exhilarated, littering, trampling, urinating hoards made their way west with visions of airplanes and boats dancing in their heads, many believed they had seen the last of an old friend. Only a few, sheltered deep in the Chicago Park District and city hall bunkers, could see the gears within gears once again begin to turn.

CHAPTER 6

PACKING UP AND HEADING NORTH

The year 1987 marked the twenty-ninth consecutive presentation of the Chicago Air and Water Show. It also began the great summer migration north from the concrete ribbon of wave-washed sidewalk and canyon of high-rises surrounding Lake Shore Park to the sandy wastes of North Avenue Beach and the surrounding green of Lincoln Park. This pulling-up-stakes decision was typically greeted by various flinty-eyed watchdog groups such as Friends of the Park.

"It makes no sense at all," said Erma Trenter, the group's director. "This is the most widely used section of Lincoln Park, and it would be horrible to bring hundreds of thousands more people into it on a summer weekend." She went on to suggest that the show was the party everyone wants to attend but no one wants to host. "We don't want it in Lincoln Park. Streeterville doesn't want it. The people on the South Side don't want it. Maybe they ought to reconsider whether they should even have an air and water show anymore."[46]

Alderman Edwin Eisendrath, recently elected to the Forty-third Ward, chipped in his objections:

> *This is a particularly bad site. In this small park area, we have the Lincoln Park Zoo, the Chicago Historical Society, the Chicago Academy of Science, the children's zoo, the playing fields and people coming to use the paddleboats in the Lincoln Park Lagoon. On the weekends, this area is impassable already, and it isn't even summer yet.*[47]

Two reasons these objections and others were shouldered aside were: 1) city hall had no intention of canceling the air and water show, and 2) in early March, Jesse Madison, the Park District's executive vice-president, and his top aide, Thomas Elzey, accepted staff input that North Avenue Beach was the most viable relocation. The mayor's office printed up a brochure of coming summer activities, and there was the decision in cold type.[48]

Still, a tug of war remained between the members of SOAR and their twenty-eight-year battle with the exponential increase of traffic and pedestrian congestion, swooping and roaring aerobatic airplanes outside their living room windows and the unhygienic habits of thousands of spectators. Better to send it over to Lincoln Park, where they were used to that sort of thing. Friends of the Park and park-side residents took vitriolic exception. But still, the shift remained in limbo.

Alderman Kathy Osterman of the Forty-eighth Ward, farther north, said they would love to have the show. Sadly, the Forty-eighth Ward between Lawrence and Granville Avenues is directly under the eastern approach to O'Hare International Airport, making that location a non-starter. Keeping the show at Lake Shore Park was no longer possible because the flight paths of the aerobatic planes took them right over Navy Pier and the Chicago Purification Plant, according to retired navy captain Jim Mahoney, a Park District advisor.

By June 10, the die was cast, and the show was moving to Lincoln Park—at least for the 1987 performance of the twenty-ninth consecutive production. But after months of bombardment by residents, fans and foes alike, Park District board member Rebecca Sive suggested that the board should decide by the fall of 1987 whether the show was more trouble than it was worth.[49]

The latest iteration arrived in July with old favorites, including the Thunderbirds and Golden Knights, plus the Harrier jet with its vertical takeoff and landing capability. Also, commercial airline pilot Julie Clark put a T34 Mentor low-wing, two-seat U.S. Navy trainer through a solo program of dazzling aerobatics—a novelty act for 1987. The Mentor was an excellent training plane prior to a pilot's move to jet aircraft.

Al Benedict, the force behind the show since its conception, predicted a crowd of 750,000 and surely curled the hair of Lincoln Park activists when he suggested that North Avenue Beach and its immediate environs could hold 500,000 *more* spectators than the Lake Shore Park/Oak Street Beach location. On July 18, the vast hordes arrived and spilled down to the hot sand, baking under ninety-degree temperatures. Makeshift shelters, umbrellas, long-sleeve shirts and wide-brim hats provided some shade, but

The Red Barons in formation, flying Stearman biplanes and advertising frozen pizza to the excited and hungry spectators along North Avenue Beach in 1987. *Courtesy Mayor's Office of Special Events.*

for all the heat and sunshine, only about seventy people had to be treated for heat-related problems.

Still, the neck-craning action was nonstop as the Red Barons put their 1940s vintage Stearman biplanes through some leisurely, but heart-stopping, precision aerobatics. The military flew a pair of C-130 Hercules transports, the KC-135 jet tanker and the USAF Thunderbirds.

"It's great watching people do things you'll never do," said one woman. Above her, Cheryl Rae Littlefield sailed though the sky, wing walking on a biplane flown by her husband, Gene, right in front of a monster C-5A Starlifter.

"I'll tell you," Cheryl said, "there's nothing like standing on the wing of a small plane with the biggest plane in the world breathing down your neck."[50]

As the Thunderbirds wrapped up the show on Sunday, despite forebodings by local residents, only one person was arrested for disorderly conduct. Most were too roasted to be disorderly and too awed by what they had seen to be disappointed. Police estimated the crowd on Saturday at 850,000, while word-of-mouth and the weather swelled that number to 1.5 million on Sunday.

Even with this overwhelming public support of the show, its future location in North Avenue Beach and the Lincoln Park area was no done deal. The debate stayed alive at least until November 25, 1987, when Mayor Harold Washington suddenly collapsed and died while sitting across from his press secretary, Alton Miller. The first term of the new regime that had brought new voices into Chicago government—voices that had heretofore been shut out—ended at 11:00 a.m. that morning. A cry went up from minorities all over the city, and the fate of the Air and Water Show was tabled until the mayor's seat could be filled.

A battle was joined immediately along the lines of the past "council wars" that had fought for and against Mayor Washington's attempted reforms. Led by "Fast Eddy" Vrdolyak, leader of the "Vrdolyak 29," the city council "Old Guard" pressed for rejection of any candidates put up by former Washington supporters. Council wars resumed with much high drama, speeches, accusations and finger pointing. In the end, Eugene Sawyer was elected by the council on December 2, 1987, to fill the job until a regular election could be organized.

Serving as a place marker, Sawyer sidestepped any decisions about the longevity of the Air and Water Show, making a statement through a spokesman that he "would not be prepared to take a position on possible changes in air show policy until he meets with the city's aviation commissioner to discuss relative levels of danger."[51]

Following the novelty of the show's first appearance at North Avenue Beach, the thirtieth presentation carried the burden of maintaining public interest in the face of considerable opposition to its new location, or even its continued existence. The 1988 show had to present continuity and stir the pot with some new ingredients. Enter Shamu, the Killer Whale.

It could never be said that a streak of whimsy was absent from the show planners' agenda. Southwest Airlines decided on May 23, 1988, to paint a few of its 737-300 airliners in the livery of Shamu the Killer Whale. This black and white mammal was the key exhibit at the SeaWorld of Texas. Painting the jet liner to resemble the famous whale was a dual promotion deal, and who at the Chicago Air and Water Show could resist a flyby from "Shamu-One?"[52]

The 1988 show also featured a return of the Canadian Snowbirds and their nine-plane flight demonstration team. Their crisp military maneuvers were balanced by the flight poetry of the French Connection husband and wife team and the swooping aerobatics of the Ray Ban Golds' Pitts specials. Cheryl Littlefield climbed onto Gene's top wing once again as

In the late 1980s, North Avenue Beach allowed parachutists to arrive on sand instead of being dunked in the water. *Courtesy Chicago Park District.*

their Stearman biplane sputtered though rolls and wingovers only five hundred feet from shore. The Golden Knights parachute team from Fort Bragg was able to enjoy landing on dry sand instead of splashing into Lake Michigan.

At age thirty, the Air and Water Show had become almost the elder statesman of summer events—trumped only by Venetian Night, which was two years older and still gliding serenely down the lakefront every year. Then the Park District moved in to support the growing production, and with success, the higher-ups got to attach their names to a winner.

Besides the U.S. Marine Corps Harrier V-STOL jet fighter, the 1986 B1-B Lancer bomber added the roar of its four General Electric F101-GE-102 turbofan engines—each capable of three thousand pounds of thrust—to the thunder above the trees and sand.[53] A beach control center wired into a four-mile radius circle around the performance area kept track of the big bomber and the other acts as they entered and exited the stage.

Safety had become an overriding concern for the FAA and the Park District early on in the productions. Even though the imaginary "box" created by orange-tarped boats and buoys bobbing on the water now had more elbowroom from the constrictions of the Lake Shore Park location, strict flight rules were maintained. Slower propeller-driven planes could

Only the equipment changed from show to show as the air-sea rescue unit performed, shown here in the 2009 show. *Courtesy Gerry Souter.*

operate as close as five hundred feet from shore, while hot jets and larger military aircraft maintained a two-thousand-foot limit. Beyond that, boaters were reined in at a buoy line three thousand feet from the sandy beach. All pilots and crews met prior to each day's performance to step through the show's rigid schedule. Air traffic at Meigs Field on Northerly Island was shut down except for staging some performers, and beyond the four-mile limit, controllers at O'Hare Airport took over sorting through the scheduled aircraft.[54]

Packing Up and Heading North

One casualty caused by the move to North Avenue Beach was the water-ski program due to the choppy waves. The skiers were sidelined or moved to the riverfront basins. In the media, the "bathing beauties" and queens also faded out of the picture as sensitivity to women's rights replaced "leg art" with women's accomplishments. While water once dominated the show and then became equal to the air performers, by 1988 it had slipped to strictly between-acts fodder when the waves took away the ski jumpers and lower sight lines for the North Avenue Beach spectators made the boat and jet ski performers hard to see. The Coast Guard air-sea rescue and the fireboat water cannon demonstrations remain to the present.

But with all the precautions, monitoring and strict timing rules, the hue and cry over safety did not go away. Alderman of the Forty-second Ward Burton F. Natarus demanded that the air shows be stopped because of a "potential loss of human life." Natarus claimed that after studying shows in Europe—and one in particular that killed forty-nine spectators—there was no safe way to hold such shows in the supersonic age. He argued:

> I've watched films, studied other air show disasters and have concluded that it's simply too dangerous to have these shows here. I don't think we could forgive ourselves if one of these planes went haywire and into a crowd or the waterworks.

The council member's fear of falling aircraft was nudged aside by the board and officers as "unfounded." According to executive vice-president of the board Jesse Madison:

> Whenever these very popular shows are planned, the first concern has always been the issue of safety. That's why we have it out over the lake, with maneuvers done in a north–south fashion. If, God forbid, something should happen to one of the planes in these shows, it would happen in the water, not in the crowd.

The year 1989 saw a thawing of the Cold War between the United States and the Soviet Union. The threadbare Communist philosophy was replaced by awareness that the tactics of the old regime could be repurposed so that those who held power could now also make a lot of money as capitalists. The old-line apparatchiks were amazed. As the former Soviet Union fell apart, with former commissars scrambling to elbow their way into stocks, bonds and petro-rubles and selling off their obsolete army and navy to third

Called "Fat Albert"—named after a Bill Cosby childhood character—this Blue Angels C-130 support aircraft became part of the show, with a jet-assisted takeoff and low flybys. *Courtesy Mayor's Office of Special Events.*

world countries, in Chicago, the Air and Water Show scrambled to amp up its attractions. It was a brave new world. One American at a Moscow cocktail party asked a Russian general with a wall of medals running down his chest if it would be possible to fly a brand-new MiG-29 jet interceptor in the Chicago Air and Water Show. The general smiled, sipped and said, "I can lobby a little bit."[55]

If this sounds like a heaping helping of hubris, the request fit perfectly with the "new and improved" thirty-second staging of the big show. There were many sighs of relief and smiles at city hall in April as the new mayor, Richard M. Daley, took over his father's former domain, and old family names once more began to fill the patronage ranks. Daley predicted an entirely new era for the city. This look into the future would affect the Air and Water Show, which had settled into a comfy sameness.

As if rising to the challenge, instead of running out of gas, the Chicago Park District topped up the tank by signing with the MDM Group, a Northbrook, Illinois marketing and talent procurement agency headed by Mickey Markoff. The largely military recruitment slant of previous shows

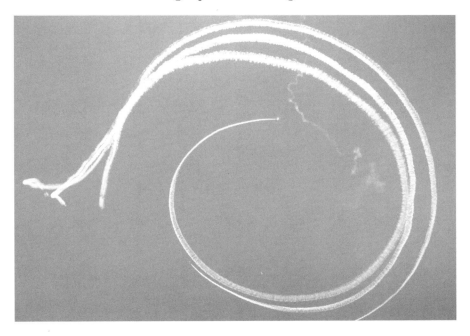

Spiral smoke trails give some idea of the maneuvers of this stunt plane for the North Avenue Beach audience. *Courtesy Mayor's Office of Special Events.*

suddenly acquired lots of civilian helpmates with their own products to sell. Stretching from Randolph Street to North Avenue Beach, volleyball teams pounded sand on the beaches, champion water-skiers flaunted their skills beneath floating kite flyers, lifesaving teams from several different countries competed for prizes and powerboats from sixteen countries raced down the Chicago River. Hovercraft huffed and puffed from water to land and back, and an entertainment center was established on a sand pile across from North Pier. Add to this the USAF Thunderbirds, the Army Golden Knights, Coast Guard rescue helicopters, B-1 bombers and a mad collection of aerobatic pilots in vintage aircraft and Chicago was turned into a weekend fun fair.

For all that entertainment, it was worth renaming the event the Budweiser Air and Water Show.

Economics drove the decision to go for broke, with commercial sponsors picking up the tab. The price of the show had escalated from $88 in 1959 to $200,000 in 1988. For the last few years, the city had shouldered the costs as part of its operating budget, drawing heavily on the taxpayer-funded military demonstration, which returned significant recruiting success

Near the beginning of his twenty-two years announcing the Chicago Air and Water Show, Herb Hunter is shown here in USAF uniform in the 1980s. He began his association with the show flying a KC-135 jet tanker. *Courtesy Chicago Park District.*

to the participating armed forces. The military dependency increased following the Vietnam conflict when Pentagon policy shifted to an all-volunteer military. Markoff's group went straight for the deepest pockets when it began sounding out cosponsors for the million-plus live captive audience, which had been seasoned over thirty-one years to expect fun and excitement. The line quickly formed and included: Midway Airlines, Budget Rent A Car, Coca-Cola, Ameritech and Polaroid, in addition to the brand-savvy crowd from Budweiser. When the speedboats roared down the Chicago River, they raced beneath the banners of the Fruit of the Loom Formula 1 Grand Prix.

The "naming rights" advertising grab was just building up steam in the United States on a grand scale for bowl games, tennis tournaments, horse races and human races. Stadiums and large civic projects, as well as vanity addresses such as One Standard Oil Place, had been sprouting up since

A USAF F-10 Warthog buzzes the crowd as one of the ugliest and most deadly weapons in our aerial arsenal. *Courtesy Mayor's Office of Special Events.*

1966, when Anheuser-Busch renamed Sportsman's Park, home of the St. Louis Cardinals, Busch Memorial Stadium after one of its brands of beer. Need we even mention the BMW Championship golf tournament or the Cialis Western Open?

By the late 1980s, commercial advertising was part of the fabric of America's lifestyle. Enduring the peddling of an erectile dysfunction remedy has become a small price to pay for watching Tiger Woods sink a fifteen-foot birdie on the eighteenth hole. The same accommodation held true for aerobatic airplanes and fast boats. Instead of shifting the costs of the show to Chicagoans in order to ensure its survival, the Park District embraced commercialism and carved up any profits with Markoff. While that Faustian deal soured some folks who still believed that the Olympics is all about amateur athleticism, it cemented the Air and Water Show in place for future generations.

Mickey Markoff is a Glenview native and the brother of *Chicago Sun Times* columnist and financial analyst Terry Savage. In 1986, he formed the MDM Group and introduced himself as a race promoter to the American Power Boat Association's offshore racing commissioner. Markoff claimed that

Water-skiers in tutus show off their skills in a lakefront program. *Courtesy Chicago Park District.*

he could provide sponsors for boat races. He invited the commissioner to Chicago for a meeting and then called the father of a friend, public relations wizard Aaron Cushman, to ask a favor. Since Markoff had no office, he borrowed a conference room, a secretary and the reputation that went with Cushman's PR name to make his pitch.

Parlaying his gift for chutzpah and hyperbole, he approached the Chicago Park District with the American Power Boat Association in his pocket to pitch a public/private partnership to offset the costs of the Air and Water Show with sponsorships. Any profits would be split with his 20 percent commission. Since Budweiser had been successfully fielding its Bud Lite Formula 1 Boat Racing Team, water sports were resuscitated, and a Formula 1 race series was added, along with the Budweiser name above the show title. Following thereafter came the Midway Airlines water-ski exhibition, the Ameritech Mobile Communications jet ski competition, the Budget Rent A Car lifeguard competition, the Polaroid photo contest, Marshall Field's beauty pageant (political correctness be damned), the Coca-Cola hovercraft exhibition and the Fruit of the Loom Formula 1 Power Boat Grand Prix.

In addition, Markoff lined up an official television station (WGN) and an official hotel (Sheraton Plaza), and the official lottery (the Illinois State Lottery) ran a special drawing for the show.

Each of the sponsors agreed to an investment in cash or trades (free air time or hotel rooms) in return for a predetermined amount of exposure as audited by Joyce Julius & Associates. The Michigan firm was tasked with counting the number of times the sponsor's logo appeared in focus on television, the number of times the Budweiser name was mentioned in the coverage and the number of people who drove by a billboard promoting the Budweiser Air and Water Show. If any projected exposure numbers fell short, Markoff promised refunds.

The increased boating events required a different venue than the wave-tossed North Avenue Beach. The Formula 1 powerboat events and jet ski and hovercraft events were started off by the powerboat races at 1:30 p.m. on Saturday in the turning basin between Randolph Street and the Chicago River.[56]

Another new venue was the Bud Beach Club at McClurg Court and North Water Street, which offered sand, a swimming pool and volleyball courts—and "This Bud's for you!"

The year 1989 set the bar for the next twenty years. Though the number of performers varied and the "air" performances were the big draw, everyone in the city knew the show would be impressive, exciting and worth the parking/walking jams and would always show off something new and usually surprising.

Eighteen Formula 1 Grand Prix powerboats churned around the turning basin, blasting their un-muffled engines and sending up the crowd-pleasing rooster tails of lake water. Those engines were capable of speeds up to 140 miles per hour but topped out—because of the small track—at about one hundred miles per hour. As one racer put it, "Kind of like putting race horses on a dog track." Stars on Water, from Winter Haven, Florida, skied on bare feet, went airborne on delta kites, built human pyramids and soared over floating jump platforms. Hovercraft and their movement on columns of downward-forced air were still new enough to be amazing as they skimmed the surface of the water and climbed the sand bank at speeds up to 40 miles per hour.

But it was still the eye-shading, neck-craning, finger-pointing discovery of yet another flight demonstration that brought the biggest gasps and cheers. Over the two days, 1.5 million spectators gaped at the huge B-1 bomber rumbling overhead and were transfixed by the precision of the Lima Lima

Lima Lima, partly because it was originally a local aerobatic team based in Naperville, was a show fixture. *Courtesy Mayor's Office of Special Events.*

Flight of six Beech T-34 Mentor prop planes as they performed classic aerobatics, twisting and turning like one plane.

The Lima Lima team flew the first night display at the Chicago Air and Water show in the late 1990s. Lima Lima pilot Bill Cherwin recalled:

> *We were at one of Rudy* [Malnati's] *parties on a Friday night at the Como Inn, and he calls me over—it's about eight o'clock at night—and he says, "Bill, do you think you could fly right now?" I looked at it, twilight, and said, "Yeah, it would go good." So he says, "Why don't we do a twilighter tomorrow night over Navy Pier." So we did the very first night show, and by the time we got on, there were delays, and it was totally dark by the time we flew. We went with it because we light each other up and we were going to see how it flew and if it went okay, then we were going to continue. But if it looked at all iffy, anytime, anybody on the team could call it off. But it went well.*
>
> *We had twelve landing lights and were spread out in formation. For night shows we stole an idea from another performer and we put light on the tail that shines back into our smoke trail. It doesn't light up the smoke trail very far. It goes into the smoke, looks like an afterburner. So that's a little twist to our night act. We fly around and do a fifteen- to*

twenty-minute night act; it's very popular, unique, it's a hell of a look and not hard to do.

The 1989 lakefront performance also featured the perennial Golden Knights parachuting down from 12,500 feet trailing plumes of red smoke. They executed free-fall maneuvers at speeds of 150 miles per hour before popping their canopies. Spectators admired the Dave Dacy air show. The veteran pilot performed barrel rolls and other skywriting stunts in a clipped-wing Bucker BU-133S Jungmeister, one of twenty such planes designed in Germany. This stilt-landing-gear biplane was flown to the United States aboard the dirigible *Hindenburg* in 1936 to compete in the Cleveland air races. The exotic Jungmeister was powered by a 165-horsepower Warner Scarab engine and was considered to be the premier stunt plane of its day.

The Chicago Hang Gliding Organization flew expert hang gliders dropped from between three thousand and two thousand feet above the ground to land on a beach target. Contrasting to the free-fall of the gliders, the USAF supplied the B-1 bomber and the F-4 Phantom II jet fighter. The new Midway Airlines' McDonnell Douglas MD-87 twin-engine, short-medium-range airliner soared across the lake's knife-edge horizon.

A pilot wrings out an F-16 Falcon fighter in a solo pass before joining up with the delta formation. *Courtesy Gerry Souter.*

The Air Force Thunderbirds, now in their thirty-seventh year, supplied the finale. The six-member demonstration team flew F-16 Falcon jets painted red, white and blue. Their final Delta pass down the lakefront, trailing smoke, was a fitting end and a memorial to all those affected by fifty-four years of the Cold War of bluff and nerves. On November 9, 1989, the Berlin Wall was officially opened to the West, symbolically ending that war and signaling the dissolution of the Soviet Union.

The Chicago Air and Water Show had become more than a local thrill event. It was the longest-running free show of its kind in the United States. It also became a symbol of America's capitalist philosophy and lifestyle, demonstrating the constant reaching for new goals at many different levels and a celebration of the pride in achievement. The show became an international event, flying the flags of many nations. Tracing back to its origin in 1911, when the world embraced the phenomenon of powered, controllable flight at the International Aviation Meet and Chicago took its place as America's aviation hub, now the Air and Water Show held up another mirror to the world's latest generation.

Over the next ten years, the Chicago Park District Air and Water Show settled even more firmly into its summertime niche as an entertainment highlight, along with the classic Venetian Night, the Taste of Chicago and the Jazz and Blues Fests. With its new sponsors, its menu of attractions grew, as did its audiences, which were never less than a million and approached two million quite often. With this number of active spectators, advertisers could count on maximum exposure to their product or message over the two-day weekend that cut across an ideal demographic. The number of sponsors for the 1990 show rose by 67 percent over that of 1989. The mix of patriotism with commercialism was irresistible.

The F-117A Stealth Fighter was the big star of the 1990 show, although it wasn't as fast as the supersonic strike fighters, and its weapons load was a fraction of the hot twin-engine fighter-bombers. It was an odd little plane, all angles and corners, and was virtually invisible to radar. Like most of the latest fighters, it was less stable in flight than the Wright Brothers Flyer of 1903, but its computer corrected that problem faster than the reflexes of any human pilot. With a development cost of $22.5 billion and an individual aircraft cost of $106 million, the design created at the Northrop Aircraft Company's top-secret "Skunk Works" had a lot to prove. The Stealth Fighter appeared like the first British tank in World War I or the German Me-262 jet in World War

II—it revolutionized military aerial warfare. And it flew over the hundreds of thousands of mesmerized spectators crowding Chicago's lakefront.

Six months later, when Operation Desert Storm was unleashed to liberate the country of Kuwait, the Stealth Fighter "did not appear" over Iraq and still devastated Saddam Hussein's military infrastructure.

In 1991, the Thunderbirds made their third consecutive flight over the city, but it was the guests of honor who took center stage. Surviving members of the famed Tuskegee Airmen, the 332nd Fighter Group, were on hand to receive the respect—long overdue—for their World War II record. As the only all-African American fighter squadron begrudgingly assigned because of a shortage of pilots to protect our bombers flying against Germany, they flew their red-tail P-51 Mustangs and never lost a single bomber to German fighter interceptors.

Operation Desert Storm had concluded with unexpected speed during the opening months of the year, and now an M-1 Abrams tank, a Bradley Fighting Vehicle, a Patriot Missile system and an array of combat equipment were on display at Chicago's lakefront. A SEAL (Sea, Air and Land) U.S. Navy combat team rappelled from a helicopter onto North Avenue Beach, secured its position and then was swept back up clinging to a dangling rope. One of the team members joked about the Golden Knights parachute team, which was also on the day's performance bill, referring to the rival service as the "Golden Cupcakes."[57]

And if somehow spectators missed the sponsorship/patriotism theme, they could find a clue in the dozens of manufacturer decals layered on Al Unser's winning Indianapolis 500 race car on display in the park with an F-16 Fighting Falcon aircraft in red, white and blue paint.

Once again, Budweiser held the naming rights for the Chicago Air and Water Show, 1992 edition. This year, the Italian flight demonstration team, Frecce Tricolori, once more visited the sky above the city. To greet them and add to the international atmosphere, the Italian ambassador, Boris Biancheri, was on hand. The U.S. Navy Blue Angels returned to the show in 1992 after a three-year absence. But the powerboating interest brought new excitement to the lakefront as the course was lengthened and the boats' exposure to the crowd was increased. One boater, Elmer Tabor, the show's water operations director, regarded the racers as

a bunch of crazies with a lot of money. The boats will race from one hundred to six hundred feet from shore, traveling up to 100 miles per hour. You fly off a wave about fifteen feet into the air. The boat literally flies from

The U.S. Navy Blue Angels roar inverted above boats off North Avenue Beach. *Courtesy Mayor's Office of Special Events.*

the water up. That's fun. Then you have to land. That isn't fun. Your teeth chatter, your spine tingles and it feels like your brains are bouncing inside your helmet. Then the water comes into your face. It's like a fire hydrant being directed right at you.[58]

While the Pentagon cast a flinty eye on the secession of Bosnia and Herzegovina from the provinces of Yugoslavia—resulting in the new term, "ethnic cleansing"—and smokers rejoiced over Nicoderm (the first patch for quitting the habit), 1992 pitted Bill Clinton against George H.W. Bush for the presidency.

At the Chicago Air and Water Show, the women showed up in force behind howling engines and vigorous G-forces in the aerobatics demonstrations. Susan Dacy from Harvard, Illinois, took a rebuilt version of the Great Lakes biplane through its paces behind a 180-horsepower Lycoming power plant. Pilot Joanne Osterud, holder of the world's record for flying upside-down, followed her, pushing around a scary Ultimate 10-300S. This design by Gordon Price was originally an upgrade to the Pitts Special clipped-wing biplane. The closed cockpit stunt plane twists and turns through the sky behind a 300-horsepower engine.[59] And finally came Jan Jones, a U.S.

Smoke trails mark the path of this stunt plane above North Avenue Beach. *Courtesy Mayor's Office of Special Events.*

Nationals winner at the controls of a Pitts Special S2S biplane. Besides her usual routine of aerobatics in the hot little plane, she added the lomcevak to her repertoire.

Lomcevak, pronounced "LOHM-sheh-vock," is Czechoslovakian for "headache" but is also called "lump-lump," or the more colloquial "Drunken Bum." The maneuver appears to be an out-of-control tumble, nose over tail and wingtip over wingtip, dousing the sky with gyrations of smoke until the plane is recovered from the nose-down position with power on the throttle. There are as many variations of this extreme aerobatic move as there are skilled pilots who can perform it.[60]

Also added to the more stirring moments was a flyby from pilot Vlado Lenoch in a World War II P-51 Mustang, considered by many experts to be the finest fighter plane in that war. Lenoch and his P-51 would become a regular feature in the show as part of the "Heritage" flight showcasing at least four classic fighters from different historical periods in air combat.

Replacing the Golden Knights in '92 was the Liberty Parachute Team, a group of expert professional parachutists who bailed out at nearly ten thousand feet and spiraled down, trailing colored smoke "candy canes." They also managed to unfurl and control a twenty-five-hundred-square-foot American flag.

Three planes in a Heritage flight show the F-15 Eagle, P-51 Mustang and F-10 Warthog. *Courtesy Mayor's Office of Special Events.*

While 1993's show was virtually a mirror image of the 1992 production, 1994 offered a few departures and one big change.

Team America flew the Italian SIAI Marchetti F-260, a hot small-attack trainer that held world speed records in its class. The three two-seater, enclosed-cockpit aerobatic planes performed more than fifty maneuvers in fifteen minutes to an original music score with their radio transmissions broadcast over the shore speakers. The F-260 saw service as a combat plane in a number of third world skirmishes.

This thirty-sixth version of the show also saw an all-navy event as the Blue Angels did their usual tight, hair-raising show, but this time the parachute team was also all-navy. The SEAL Leapfrogs bailed out from high altitude, maneuvered on the way down to a wet landing and waded ashore in combat gear. All of the action was described to the crowd by chief announcer Sandy Sanderson, doing a job that required a strong

A short-nose version of the Blue Angels F11F-1 Tiger supersonic fighter. *Courtesy Naval Aviation Museum, Pensacola, FL.*

voice and a lot of aircraft knowledge. In a *Chicago Tribune* interview, Sanderson talked about his attitude and his work after thirty years of experience and a half dozen air shows a year. "When I was a kid, I had an incredible appetite for airplane information. One of the first books I bought was *An Air Craft Spotter's Guide*," said Sanderson, who started flying when he was eleven with his uncle's guidance.

> *How do you entertain the masses of people who know little about airplanes without boring the aircraft aficionados? On the other hand, how do you inform the aficionados without confusing the neophytes? Sometimes, it's a hard line to walk because both audiences are important. But I try to keep it at a level where everyone has no trouble understanding what I'm talking about.*
>
> *I'll start out by saying, "Here comes an AT6 powered with a Pratt & Whitney 1340 engine with a nine-cylinder radial and 600 hp." That's for the person who knows a lot about planes. Then I'll say, "But don't let those letters and numbers fool you, folks. The AT6 stands for advanced trainer, sixth model. And Pratt & Whitney is the manufacturer of the radial, or round, airplane engine with nine cylinders that has a 1,340-cubic-inch*

displacement. In other words, folks, this is an airplane they train people in after they advance their skills."

If I have time, I'll say: "If you have a Ford Escort, you have a four-cylinder engine with so many cubic inches and so much horsepower." [That's] *something that will satisfy even schoolchildren.*

He often threw a few facts out again for the airplane buffs. "I'll talk about trivia and history, such as the differences in the same plane used by the U.S. Navy and the U.S. Air Force."

Over the years, Sanderson had been a crop-duster, commercial pilot and producer and announcer of an air show act he created with a partner. He worked full time as an air show announcer. He now flies solely for his enjoyment. "I make four or five flights a week," says Sanderson, who lives in Santa Ana, California.[61]

The big change began in 1994 and carried across to 1995 as the Mayor's Office of Special Events took over control of the Air and Water Show from the Chicago Park District, according to John Trick, director of operations and air show manager. The transfer also terminated the relationship with Mickey Markoff and his MDM Group, which brought sponsors to the event in 1989. With sponsorship, the cost burden had been lifted from municipal budgets to be replaced by a blazing new and unfamiliar concept: profits.

What made the 1995 show distinctive was the announcement by the mayor's office that the Air and Water Show would bookend—along with the Jazz Fest—the 1996 Democratic Convention. Since the 1968 Windy City convention debacle, Chicago had worn the scarlet letter as far as national politics were concerned. Richard J. Daley's son set out to change that bitter perception.

Winning the prize for "something new and different," Team America flashed overhead in three red, white and blue Fouga CM-170 Magister jet trainers designed in the 1950s by Pierre Mauboussin, who was noted for stuffing jet engines into glider frames, as noted by the aircraft's odd V-tail. The plane distinguished itself as a ground-attack fighter for Israel during the 1967 Six-Day War and served with many third world and second tier nations; the Belgian air force nicknamed it "the Whistling Turtle."

Scheduled to kick off convention week, the Air and Water Show offered an advance blast of hot air from the afterburners of the Blue Angels. They once again gave a good account of their skills, piloting their F-18 Hornets and hammering the crowd with thirty-two thousand pounds of thrust—roughly one pound of thrust per pound of weight for each plane. The Blues

The Blue Angels celebrated their fiftieth anniversary in 1996. *Courtesy Mayor's Office of Special Events.*

celebrated their fiftieth anniversary while Chicago welcomed the thirty-eighth iteration of the show.

The following summer brought over two million Chicagoans and visitors to the lakeshore, where the Thunderbirds prowled, the Stearman biplanes mirrored the T-Birds in the name of Red Baron Frozen Pizza in slow-motion ballet and the Sea-doos splashed all over the sands of North Avenue Beach. The big star of the 1997 show was the B-2 bomber. The B-2 is just plain frightening. While the B-1 blasted engine noise across the North Shore, the B-2 arrived silently. Its General Electric turbofan engines are buried in its wing/fuselage—a modern version of the YB-49 "Flying Wing" experimental bomber of the late 1940s. Its surfaces are made of composite materials painted with a radar signal–reducing compound. A two-man crew is responsible for a forty-two-thousand-pound maximum load of weapons.[62] But its menace lies in stealth, and even on a sunny, seventy-degree day, its flight profile on edge makes it hard to see—until it banks, and then you can view the true strangeness of its unique hooded design. Presentation of the B-2 bomber helped celebrate the fiftieth anniversary of the United States Air Force.

One of Chicago's own was at the controls of the popular B-1 bomber when it roared over the beach. Air force captain John Lyons flew his B-1

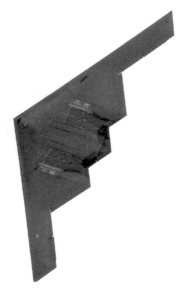

Above: Four Stearman biplanes perform their stunts against a blue Lake Michigan sky. *Courtesy Mayor's Office of Special Events.*

Left: Until the B-2 Stealth bomber banked in a turn, its edge-on silhouette was difficult for audiences to see. *Courtesy Mayor's Office of Special Events.*

Lancer above friends, family and 1.1 million cheering fans at 480 miles per hour on Saturday. Just twenty years earlier, he had watched the Air and Water Show at Lake Shore Park, imagining himself flying above the lake. Now, after landing and being whisked back to North Avenue Beach, he was signing autographs, while his sister, Jody Harvel of Crystal Lake, watched.

"I never thought I'd see him fly a B-1 bomber in the air show, and I didn't think I'd see him sign autographs," Harvel said. "I'm not nervous watching him fly because I know he's good at what he does."[63]

Sometimes, the Air and Water Show produced collateral effects on Chicagoland. On Sunday afternoon, during the 1998 performance, Brad Ausmus of the Houston Astros stood at the plate in Wrigley Field waiting for the ball from Chicago Cubs pitcher Steve Trachsel. As the pitcher loosed his spheroid toward the batter, an F-18 Hornet jet hammered over the grandstands, traveling from home plate toward center field. Everyone in the stadium levitated as the hot, low pass burned across the sky and was gone. In the vacuum-like silence of its wake, umpire Jeff Nelson ruled the ball now in the catcher's mitt to be a "no pitch." With the wallop of the jet's surprise arrival and departure, he had missed the call. Trachsel then pitched a fit, claiming he had thrown a strike. Nelson folded his arms, and that was that. The count remained at one ball, one strike. Ahead of the count, Asmus socked the next toss for a single that scored a run, which unleashed a parade of runs ending in a 13–3 Astros victory.[64]

According to FAA safety officer Jerry Wyatt:

> *Usually, since the jet team is in town anyway during the Air Show, they do occasionally, by coincidence, happen to be in the vicinity of Wrigley Field about the time the National Anthem is sung. So, as I like to point out to the military guys at my Air Show briefings, those Air Force, Navy, Marine, and Army pilots are not only* not *prohibited from flying near Wrigley Field, they are helping to* defend *it!*

One popular, hardworking spectator was absent from the 1998 show and that was Donald Jens, who, along with Al Benedict, had kept the show going for forty years. Jens died on February 2, 1998, at age seventy-two. He had worked for the show for twenty-six years, retiring in 1991.

In 1999, when the USAF Thunderbirds landed at the new staging airport in Gary, Indiana, they piled into vans with their families and personal gear for their ride into Chicago and were promptly pulled over by the Indiana State Tollway Authority Police. Being escorted by a phalanx of Gary Police

A pair of Blue Angels roars over some of the sailboat fleet watching the show from Lake Michigan. *Courtesy Mayor's Office of Special Events.*

motorcycles did not, apparently, excuse the T-Birds from paying their tolls across the skyway. After a half hour of lip flapping between jurisdictions, the USAF Flight Demonstration Team coughed up the toll money and was allowed to proceed.[65]

This was the first year that the Gary/Chicago Regional Airport acted as host to the military aircraft for the Air and Water Show. Approximately twenty-five planes ranging from military jets to civilian stunt teams and individuals arrived on Thursday to prepare for Friday rehearsals and briefings. Bleacher stands were set up by the Gary airport administration to create a mini air show of its own with an eye on future expansion to a full-blown event.[66]

As the calendar flipped over to the new millennium, all of the pieces were in place for the next ten years of the Chicago Air and Water Show. The poster for the year 2000 wore the City of Chicago official seal across from the familiar logo of Shell Oil, the latest overall sponsor. Rudy Malnati had secured Shell sponsorship and was now the show's go-to guy. He had grown up with the show, alongside Al Benedict, during its earliest days as a day camp event at Lake Shore Park. The only change on the broadsheets from show to show would be the highlight aerobatic team: either the Thunderbirds or the Blue Angels. And even more people

The "most dangerous" AH64 Apache helicopter—so deadly in Operation Desert Storm—poses in a hover for spectators' cameras. *Courtesy Chicago Park District.*

came each summer, raising the lakefront weekend crush to over three million spectators.

The appeal of the immutable, virtually unchanging performances baffles some Chicagoans, but to many the excitement of anticipation of this grand tradition is infectious. As *Tribune* staff writer Heather Vogell reported:

> *Spectators said repeat performances—the parachutists drifting from the sky, the roaring jets, the whirring Apache helicopters—were precisely what has kept them coming back. As early as 4:45 a.m. Saturday, people were packing coolers, hoping that an early start would guarantee them a good spot for viewing the show from the beach. By noon, the blankets, chairs, tables and tents left little sand exposed. For some, the celebration of technological and military might was a chance to live the pilot's life vicariously. For others, the show evoked memories.*[67]

CHAPTER 7

THE SHOW CARRIES ON

Following the terrorist attacks in New York on September 11, 2001, many air shows and large public gatherings across the country shut down for the summer due to security concerns. The Chicago Air and Water Show was not one of them. On that Saturday morning in August 2002, the beaches and parks on the city's Lake Michigan shore exploded with rippling American flags. The drumbeat of patriotism suffused that summer weekend, even beneath cloudy skies and with rigid security procedures in place. Chicagoans took it in stride and continued their homegrown tradition that was more than forty years old.

"The show is our salute to the military. That's what this is all about," said Rudy Malnati, show director.

> Our military is often not given enough credit and sometimes it takes a tragedy for people to take notice. But the military here is always the main objective. Those whose appetite for a career in the service is whetted by the show can visit the recruiting booths that will be set up by all branches of the military or try a flight simulator. We're going to have simulators just west of Lake Shore Drive at North Avenue Beach so people can see what it's like to fly an F-15, F-18 or a Stearman, the kind the Red Barons fly.[68]

In 2005, the first Air Show accident occurred. Cruising past the North Avenue Beach crowd in a photo-op pass, the Thunderbird pilot flying in the

Above: A Blue Angels C-130 support plane, nicknamed "Fat Albert," flies over North Avenue Beach above the vast crowd and anchored boats. *Courtesy Mayor's Office of Special Events.*

Below: A Heritage flight comparing a P-51 Mustang from World War II, an F4 Phantom II from Vietnam, an F15 Eagle from Desert Storm and an F22 Raptor for the future in 2004. *Courtesy Mayor's Office of Special Events.*

The Show Carries On

A two-seat F-16 Thunderbird is waved into its parking space at the Gary Jet Center following a VIP trip on Media Day. *Courtesy Gerry Souter.*

diamond slot position below and to the rear of the other three F-16s briefly touched the bottom of a wing above him. No pilot particularly noticed the touch, but the Thunderbirds' ground observer saw it and asked for a "battle damage" check. The slot pilot, who was new in that position, looked up and saw a three-inch scratch on the F-16's lower wing panel. Then he saw that a four-foot section of rocket rail was also missing. The touch had sheared off the rail, which then arced down into the lake. The formation was still over the safety "box" marked by buoys and police boats, so no one was near the rail when it carved into the water. The Thunderbirds' flight "boss" called it a day and, for safety's sake, led the four planes back to the Gary Jet Center, where they had staged. The performance for the following Sunday was canceled.

Celebrities had been joining the agenda, but in 2008—in honor of the show's fiftieth performance—the city went all out by scheduling an additional show on Friday and threw in big-name celebrity entertainment as well. Singer Florence Henderson (also known as Carol Brady on the *Brady Bunch*) led off with the national anthem. Comedian and Chicago native Bill Murray did his part by joining one of the Golden Knights in a tandem parachute jump. An attendant cameraman recorded Murray's mugging as he skidded to a halt on the beach with relative dignity. On the beach stage,

Above: Bill Murray works the crowd at the North Avenue Beach stage after parachuting down with the Golden Knights. *Courtesy Mayor's Office of Special Events.*

Left: Gary Sinise, Chicago native and star of *CSI: NY* jams with his Lieutenant Dan Band, named after the character he played in the film *Forrest Gump. Courtesy Mayor's Office of Special Events.*

The Show Carries On

Above: In 2009, AT-6 Texan training planes perform over the lake and above Chicago's skyscrapers in an intricate smoke-trail Immelman turn to join up again. *Courtesy Gerry Souter*.

Below: Sean Tucker wrings out his red biplane with two other pilots during the fiftieth presentation of the Chicago Air and Water Show. *Courtesy Mayor's Office of Special Events*.

ED HAMILL:
LIVING THE DREAM

Strains of "America the Beautiful" fade, and the announcer tells the audience, "We'd like to thank you for watching today. We hope it's inspiring. Just as Ed reaches for his dream in the Air Force Reserve, we'd like to encourage you to reach for yours. It's up to you to continue this journey into the future. Set goals. Work hard. Never give up. And start living your dream. Get your cameras ready and give a big wave as Ed Hamill turns his Air Force Reserve biplane back to show center. Thank you. And Godspeed."

Talk to any aerobatic pilot and he will tell you it was watching other air show performers that first inspired him to learn aerobatic flying. Ed Hamill's dream was forged at the Chicago Air and Water Show when he was a child growing up in suburban Northbrook. And it was seeing the Blue Angels' and Thunderbirds' routines that made him decide to train for a career as an F-16 fighter pilot. He joined the air force and traveled, and civilian flying took a backseat.

The dream, like a loyal friend, stayed. He knew that he wanted to be in air shows, somehow. Later, in southern California, as he watched pilots like Sean Tucker and others, he noticed the impact their performances made on the audiences, especially the kids. That sealed his dream. Combining air show aerobatics and competition flying, he built up his hours and experience and eventually created his "Living the Dream" routine, sponsored by the U.S. Air Force Reserve.

The performance, coordinated with narration and music, takes the audience back one

Gary Sinise, another Chicagoan, brought his Lieutenant Dan Band, named after the legless Vietnam veteran he played in the film *Forrest Gump*. More aerobatics and a fireworks show at night rounded out the day. Blue skies, warm sun, fast boats, hyper planes and rock 'n' roll showed off the finest production to date of the free show that just would not quit.

We were lucky enough to be part of the 2009 show. We spent most of the week at the Gary Jet Center as the pilots arrived, beginning with the Thunderbirds, who rocketed above the acres of concrete and then banked into a turn until each peeled off with gear coming down to land and taxi. The red and white AeroShell AT-6 Texan flight team arrived with similar panache, as did the orange Lima Lima squadron in its T-34 Mentors. Sean Tucker sky danced for ten minutes above our heads in his considerably modified Pitts Challenger painted bright red with the Oracle logo emblazoned on the upper wing. Ed Hamill swooped in without fuss in his blue Pitts, advertising the army reserve.

Ed Hamill "Lives the Dream" every time he takes off and flies his specially choreographed program representing the U.S. Army Reserve. *Courtesy http://www. aircraftspruce.com.*

hundred years of air show flying. It starts with barnstorming routines accompanied by period music of the 1920s, continues to the '50s and '60s with rock 'n' roll, surfing songs and Broadway show tunes and finishes with high-energy sky dancing and patriotic music. Ed choreographs the routine, writes the script and mixes it in the studios. As the final words of his routine tell us, the whole purpose of his performance is to inspire others, especially the kids.

He finds his greatest challenge—whether interviews, flying the aircraft or putting the sequence together—is simply doing it right. "When people tell me I did a great job," he said. "I say, 'Work in progress, I'm working on it.'"

They were both knocked from the same mold: small stature, whipcord lean and squared away in military fashion; disciplined men with sun-washed faces and deep-creased corners to their eyes. Like the Thunderbirds, all of the pilots we met moved and talked like people who were used to controlling any situation in which they found themselves.

Herb Hunter, the show announcer for many years, is also like that. A former KC-135 tanker pilot, he still did commercial runs when he wasn't at a microphone somewhere. Hunter carried a loose-leaf binder at all times. It was the show bible: performers, schedules, the hardware they flew and talking points to use between acts. He lived by it for the weekend he spent at the beach.

Thursday was VIP Day when ordinary mortals had a chance to find out what it was like to be tossed around the sky. Co-author Janet scrambled into the rear cockpit of an AeroShell AT-6 Texan—a World War II trainer—and took off with the team for a roller-coaster half hour.

UPSIDE DOWN OVER GARY:
JANET FLIES WITH AEROSHELL

Boarding the Aeroshell Aerobatic Team's AT-6 Texan is a challenge. Servicemen who flew the World War II single-engine training aircraft certainly had enough upper-body weight to step on the wallet-sized tread and hoist themselves in. I, however, needed a push. Being a gentleman, pilot Gene McNeely stepped aside and let my husband provide the heave-ho.

"Okay, here's your headset," Gene said once I got settled. "You done this before? No? Don't worry, you'll have fun. Now, I'll get you strapped into your parachute. You won't need it, but just in case, when I give the signal, you'll stand up in the seat, and then dive, like you're diving into a pool."

Wait, I wanted to say. I don't dive. I step down the ladder and swim with my head above water. But he was already pointing out the little plastic bag in the pocket in front of me, just in case.

"You won't need this, either," he said.

He was right. I hadn't eaten all day.

"You can leave the canopy open," he shouted. "Until we reach cruising altitude."

That made sense. I'd get better photos, without scratches or reflections. In fact, it seemed silly to close it at all. Why not get the maximum thrill?

The wind whistled through my hair as the plane lifted. The engine roared. The Gary Jet Center became a tiny white rectangle. The lake off to the right sparkled in the sun. Railroad tracks and freight cars resembled children's playthings. I could stay up here forever.

Gene shouted something, but above the noise of the motor and the wind, his words were garbled. I still had the canopy open. Suddenly the little plane that let me slip the bonds of earth turned into an evil mechanical raptor. It leapt up, then down, tilted, swerved and bumped into air pockets. I wanted to grab something to hang onto—knobs and levers stuck out from all sides, but I didn't know what might happen if I touched any of them. My back stiffened, and my breath refused to come. Had I taken my blood pressure pills? If so, they weren't helping. The plane swerved again, zoomed sideways, tilted and tilted again. I was a passenger on a trackless roller coaster. At one point, I glanced up, expecting to see sky and clouds, and found myself looking at Lake Michigan. I screamed, hoping to release the tension.

"You okay back there?" Gene shouted.

"Yeah, I'm fine." Hey, I told myself. You're not a coward.

The rolls and dips continued. My back wouldn't move. My breath came in short gasps. Then, just as quickly, the plane leveled off as we headed back to the airport.

"That was great, Gene!" I shouted as we touched down.

"Really?"

Really. Would I do it again? In a heartbeat.

But next time, I'll close the canopy.

The Show Carries On

Above: The show announcer for the past twenty-two years, Herb Hunter is always "on" once he arrives at the show stage and switches on the microphone. *Courtesy Gerry Souter*.

Below: Firefighter Brian Otto was interviewed on camera before his guest flight in an F-16 Fighting Falcon piloted by a Thunderbird. *Courtesy Gerry Souter*.

Above: Hometown Hero Brian Otto, honored firefighter, gets a briefing from a Thunderbird crewman before taking off on his guest ride in the F-16. *Courtesy Gerry Souter.*

Below: All crews and pilots participating in the 2009 Air and Water Show met for a briefing by the FAA and show directors, going over every aspect of the upcoming performances in a dining room at the Hyatt McCormick Place Hotel. *Courtesy Gerry Souter.*

The previous Monday, the nominated Hometown Hero, firefighter Brian Otto, experienced barrel rolls, loops, a 9G-force turn and several other maneuvers when he rode with the Thunderbirds. Otto's mother, Trudy Schubert, had nominated him for the Thunderbird's newly established Hometown Hero contest, in which the group takes one deserving community

A diagram showing the FAA "Exhibition Box," or stage, where pilots execute their maneuvers. Buoys and boats mark the space for reference from the air. *Courtesy Federal Aviation Administration.*

member on a flight prior to a local air show. Otto had helped save a child from drowning and was selected by the T-Birds for the flight in an F-16 Fighting Falcon.

Friday was rehearsal day, and those who were lucky enough to escape their cubicles and head down to North Avenue Beach were treated to a preview of

A Thunderbird solo F-16 races past Chicago's lakefront in a high-speed pass. *Courtesy Gerry Souter.*

the weekend performance, minus the heavier crowds. Farther north, Cubs fans and players got a jolt from the Thunderbirds as they buzzed Wrigley Field during a practice run. Right fielder Kosuke Fukudome never saw it coming: "I was really shocked, and I don't think it's going to happen in Japan," he said.

At 7:30 a.m. on Saturday and Sunday, the pilots and crews gathered in a meeting room at the Hyatt McCormick Place Hotel to go over any problems experienced during Friday's rehearsal, as well as the show's scheduled arrivals and departures. They studied a graphic of the all-important show "box" that was their imaginary stage and very real safety boundaries established by the FAA safety officers.

Herb Hunter called out each performing team on the roll call, along with its start and end times and length of performance. Each team leader read its call sign; for example, the USAF F-15 Strike Eagle is "Eagle." Then came

The Show Carries On

Above: The familiar silhouette of the MiG-17 fighter, shown here in 2009 Red Bull livery, was a missile target for prowling F-4 Phantoms in Vietnam. The small, cheaply built jet could hold its own in a dogfight. *Courtesy Gerry Souter.*

Below: A pair of Extra-300 stunt monoplanes belonging to the Firebirds zooms over the crowd at the 2009 show. *Courtesy Gerry Souter.*

BILL REESMAN:
MIG-17 PILOT

As a pilot in the Vietnam War, Bill Reesman did whatever he could to bring down the Russian-built MiG-17 aircraft, with its 37mm cannon on the nose and two 23mm guns on either side. Not an easy job. "That plane really beat us up in Vietnam," he says.

Today, he has an unending love affair with the MiG he once sought to destroy.

"Now I get to play in it. I've flown over fifty-some airplanes. I have 320 combat missions," he said. "I've done airline pilot. I've done general aviation. And now I've done the stunt show flying for eighteen years. With all that experience, I love this airplane more than anything I've ever flown."

Yet his experience with his first MiG, the Chinese-built Shenyang J-5, might have discouraged another pilot from ever flying a MiG again.

"The fuel line broke, ruptured, caught fire and exploded on takeoff. I landed it with about forty feet of flame off the left side of the airplane," Reesman said. "The tail was burned off. I set a new world's record for a fifty-two-year-old man in the one-hundred-yard dash. I really wasn't scared, but I passed ten people who were running like they were terrified. And it happened right after the start of air show season."

Shortly thereafter, he and his team found a fleet of fifteen Polish MiGs in Scottsdale, Arizona. They picked out the best of the lot, put ten mechanics to work on it and he was ready to go two months later. That's because the plane's mechanism is simple, Reesman says. "It doesn't have a lot of the bells and whistles that we build into our airplanes. This airplane knows exactly what its job is and it goes and does it. It's built like a tank. I've had three crashes in MiGs—off the runway and

Bill Reesman poses with his Red Bull MiG-17 jet fighter in 2009. This plane was the backbone of the North Vietnamese air force during that conflict in the late 1960s and '70s. *Courtesy Gerry Souter.*

different things gone wrong with the airplane. I'm still here, the airplane's still here. It's a tank with a set of wings."

The plane's tight turning radius makes it perfect for air shows. Reesman can do six hundred miles an hour and never get farther than about three-quarters of a mile away from show center. His MiG Meteor Red Bull performance is the only night jet fighter aerobatic pyrotechnic act, with the afterburner shooting flames out the rear, along with the wing-mounted smoke system.

However, the aircraft's instrument panel does require some thinking. Navigation instruments are in English, but during a performance Reesman is also looking at gauges in Cyrillic and Chinese.

"I can't read them, but I know where the needles are supposed to point. So a little bit of Chinese, a little bit of American and a little bit of Polish in the cockpit."

And a pilot with imagination and a healthy respect for his aircraft.

the checklist: departure airport and time (Gary Airport, 13:45); holding point and altitude (behind crowd at five thousand feet); entering point (south) and exit point (north); and maximum altitude during the performance (fifteen hundred feet). Herb added that there was a swearing-in ceremony on Saturday for new air force recruits. The meeting concluded with Rudy Malnati's final comments: "You'll see more people here than ever before. Don't try to impress yourself or the crowd. Have a good show."

Then we left for the boat that took us out to the center of that "box," the best seats in the house if you don't mind wearing earplugs or bobbing about for a few hours. The show came off without a hitch. Seeing the trails of smoke against the panorama of the city gave a scale to the performances and a sense of speed. Concrete pillars and cliffs of glass blurred behind the wings of these sky dancers who romanced the crowd with finesse and stirred the blood with sheer power.

Unique elements included a structure-strengthened Red Bull aerobatic helicopter piloted by Chuck Aaron that amazed and confounded aficionados with impossible inside loops. Bill Reesman charged across the stage at the controls of the former darling of the North Vietnamese air force—also sponsored by Red Bull energy drink—an all-red MiG-17 jet fighter.

On Sunday, we watched from the beach as jet skiers careened over boat wakes with their rooster tails of spray that were prelude to the first flyby. On that day, the aerial performers had no lock on death-defying stunts. The only near-disaster in the 2009 show occurred during the

SEAN TUCKER:
SKY DANCER

The Thunderbirds' F-16s were parked in precision at the Gary Jet Center, their noses perfectly aligned. Suddenly a brash red Challenger II biplane zoomed over them about one hundred feet, almost taunting them to follow. It headed up, kissed the clouds, twirled into a stall and then fell backward, straight down, tail first, at one hundred miles per hour.

"Who's that guy in the red plane?" someone asked.

It was Sean Tucker, of Team Oracle, and on the Monday before the Air and Water Show, he had already practiced his routine several times and would continue to hone it until the day of the show.

"A plane may appear to be out of control," Sean said later, "but the pilot must have control all the time, whether you're flying backwards tail first for eight hundred feet in a torque roll or an eight-ten tumble centrifuge arcing tail over nose across the sky, it has to work. The air show environment is a low-level environment—there is no margin for error."

Strangely enough, it was fear that propelled him into aerobatic flying originally. When he first learned to fly, he had an underlying fear of going into a stall. He knew that someday he'd panic and kill himself, and the only way to prevent that was to attack the problem head on. He took an aerobatic course from a female aviator, and after she rolled the plane upside-down and back up, she had Sean try it. That's when he fell in love with aerobatic flight.

And he's had a healthy respect for it ever since. No matter that he is in the National Aviation Hall of Fame. The biggest challenge for him is maintaining the level of responsibility to the industry, to himself, to his family and to the air show fans. He works

Team Twangled jet ski performance. The stunt show team uses two large cabin cruisers moving side by side to create a huge double-up wave for the jet skier to perform his maneuvers. "The larger the wave, the better to thrill the fans" is the team's motto. But when rider Kyle Burtka under-rotated a barrel roll, the jet ski's hood popped and jarred loose the bilge pump wiring. Burtka hit the water with a jarring crash and was pulled under several times by the submerging watercraft. Fortunately, fellow team member Mike Niksik saw what happened, slewed his jet ski around, reached into the water and grabbed Kyle's vest, pulling him to the surface. Rescue teams got Kyle to the hospital, where he was treated and then released.

Sean Tucker with his Custom Challenger aircraft sponsored by Oracle computer software. *Courtesy Team Oracle, http://www. poweraerobatics.com.*

out new routines each year, but very little changes once show season starts. Practice takes over, and he'll go through the routine one hundred times.

While other pilots prefer the hi-tech aircraft, Sean has a special love for his Oracle Challenger II's fabric and wood design. "It creates a nuance with the air," he said. "Whenever you're twirling or spinning through the sky or tumbling, its slight control inputs to allow the plane to do that, and the more feel you get from it, the more precise you can be in these aerobatic figures. Also for air show flying, there's a romance to a biplane."

It's obvious to anyone who meets him that Sean loves every minute of the air show experience.

"It's a tremendous metaphor of freedom," he says. "It's a tremendous metaphor of daring. It's a tremendous metaphor of passionate existence, and so I feel very privileged to be able to do this. It amazes me when I taxi back in front of the crowd to see that happiness, because flight means something very special to people."

Later, Burtka said, "Lake Michigan does get pretty rough at times and today was one of them. It's the price you pay for the show."

Above the waves, the aircraft were cutouts against an overcast sky. Forbidden by the rules to penetrate the clouds, the performers brought down their "low show" limits. No one seemed to mind. If you can't deal with changing weather, you live in the wrong city. That's the nature of the Chicago Air and Water Show. Even as the first raindrops fell, people still arrived. By the time the Thunderbirds howled overhead, bringing down the curtain, more people had replaced those headed north, west and south toward home. Just to catch a piece of the action, to witness a level of skill and daring few people possess, has always been enough.

Since those "aeroplane drivers" of 1911 took off in their wood, wire and fabric creations from Grant Park, Chicago spectators have lifted off with them. There is something about witnessing supersonic flight or watching others challenge the unpredictable Lake Michigan waves that encourages our own dreams to soar. The performers know this; that's why they continue to be part of the Air and Water Show year after year. As Sean Tucker put it, "I want to share the magic...by inspiring and thrilling the audience. I want them to go away saying that the Air and Water Show was one of the most engaging days of their lives."

NOTES

CHAPTER 1

1. Carroll F. Gray, "Cicero Flying Field: Origin, Operation, Obscurity and Legacy, 1891–1916," *World War I Aero Magazine–Journal of the Early Aeroplane*, http://www.lincolnbeachey.com/cicart.html.
2. http://csudh.edu/1910airmeet/event/, California State University Dominguez Hills Campus.
3. Frank Coffyn, *History of Flight* (New York: Simon & Schuster, 1962), 154.

CHAPTER 2

4. Christopher Lynch, *Chicago's Midway Airport: The First Seventy-five Years* (Chicago: Lake Claremont Press, 1966), 33–34.
5. http://EzineArticles.com/?expert=Duncan_Rice; http://EzineArticles.com/?Wingfoot-Air-Express—The-First-Airship-Disaster&id=1014840.
6. Chicago History Museum, http://www.chicagohs.org/popup.html.
7. Airships Historical Site, http://www.airships.net/lz127-graf-zeppelin.
8. Chicago Park District *Carnival of the Lakes*, brochure, 1934.

CHAPTER 3

9. *Time* magazine online, http://www.time.com/time/magazine/article/0,9171,892754,00.html.

10. Ibid.

11. *Chicago Daily Tribune*, "Crowds Watch Park District Water Show," August 6, 1962, 12.

12. Rudy Malnati interview, June 30, 2009.

13. Gerry Souter, "Tigers, Cougar, Angels in Sky Over Yuma," *Yuma News Enterprise, Yuma Daily Star, Los Angles Times*, February 1964.

14. *Chicago Tribune*, "Chutists Star in High Dive at Aquatic Show," August 30, 1964, B3.

CHAPTER 4

15. 1962–67 Amphicar, http://www.conceptcarz.com/vehicle/z2635/1966-Amphicar-770.aspx.

16. *Chicago Tribune*, "Lake Festival Launched by King Neptune," August 16, 1966, 2.

17. *Naval Aviation News*, "In Memorium – Captain Richard A. Schram," *USNR* (August 1969).

18. Citizens for a Better Environment report, http://www.uic.edu/depts/lib/specialcoll/services/rjd/findingaids/CBEb.html.

19. Referred to as "Formosa" in the *Chicago Tribune* reference.

20. Dave Condon, "In the Wake of the News," *Chicago Tribune*, August 9, 1969, 1.

21. Terry Denton interview, October 21, 2009, Arlington Heights, Illinois.

22. Michael Killian, "Will the Mayor Swim, Col Reilly?" *Chicago Tribune*, August 8, 1971, A5.

23. *Chicago Tribune*, "King Neptune to Preside Over Lakefront Gala," August 10, 1972, W6.

24. http://www.bettertrades.net/stock-market-crashes/1973-1974-stock-market-crash.asp.

25. Thunderbirds history, http://thunderbirds.airforce.com/index.html.

26. *Chicago Tribune*, "Pigeons Score Hit on Lake Fete," August 12, 1973, 26.

27. *Chicago Tribune*, "40 Nags in Parade Don't Horse Around," August 12, 1973, 25.

28. http://www.steenaero.com/PittsS1/history.cfm.

29. Ibid.; Rudy Malnati interview.

30. "Stunt Pilot Repairs Plane, Then Crashes," *Byran Times*, September

24, 1977, http://news.google.com/newspapers?id=E14RAAAAIBA J&sjid=FYgDAAAAIBAJ&pg=3837,698217&dq=air+show+disaster (accessed July 2009).

CHAPTER 5

31. Richard Roeper, "Col. Jack Reilly Dies," *Chicago Sun Times*, July 5, 1988.
32. http://www.globalsecurity.org/military/systems/aircraft/c-5-design.htm.
33. Canadian Reds, http://www.flying-colors.org/CFAMR.
34. John W.R. Taylor, *Jane's All the World's Aircraft, 1988–89* (Coulsdon, UK: Jane's Defence Data, 1988).
35. NTSB Accident Report, http://www.ntsb.gov/ntsb/brief2.asp?ev_id=2 0001212X21058&ntsbno=MIA00FA172A&akey=1.
36. McDonnell Douglas F-15 Streak Eagle Fact Sheet, National Museum of the United States Air Force.
37. *Chicago Tribune*, "Inc. Column," June 6, 1983, 18.
38. Stevenson Swanson, "725,000 Get a Lift Watching Air Show," *Chicago Tribune*, July 18, 1983, 1.
39. BD-5J Acrostar Microjet, http://www.aerospaceweb.org/question/planes/q0256.shtml.
40. Ben Holden, "Breeze, Back-ups Fail to Ground Air Show," *Chicago Tribune*, July 14, 1985.
41. Bonnie McGrath, "Every Year Crowds Jam Lakefront to Watch Aerial Feats of Derring-Do—High Rises Have Front Row Seat," *Chicago Tribune*, July 31, 1985.
42. Mitchell Locin and William Recktenwald, "Streeterville Takes Cover As Air Show Blitz Looms," *Chicago Tribune*, July 11, 1986.
43. Alpha Jet description, http://www.fighter-planes.com/info/alphajet.htm.
44. http://www.deagel.com/Long-Range-Attack-Aircraft/F-111F-Aardvark_a000758001.aspx.
45. Rob Karwath, "Glass Houses Throw Stones at Air Show," *Chicago Tribune*, July 13, 1986.

CHAPTER 6

46. Robert Davis, "Moving of Lake Air Show Creates Roar," *Chicago Tribune*, May 14, 1987.
47. Ibid.
48. Ibid.

49. *Chicago Tribune*, "Air Show Moving to North Ave. Site," June 10, 1987.

50. Jacquelyn Heard, "Their Marriage Has Its Ups and Downs," *Chicago Tribune*, August 12, 1987.

51. Zay N. Smith, "Park Boss Still Favors Show," *Chicago Sun Times*, August 31, 1988.

52. Flight Global, Flight Image of the Day, "SW Airlines Paints 737 to Resemble Whale," http://www.flightglobal.com/blogs/aircraft-pictures/2009/05/on-this-day-in-1988-southwest.html.

53. USAF B-1B Lancer bomber, http://www.airforce-technology.com/projects/b-1b.

54. David C. Rudd, "Performers Flirt with Danger but Skill Keep the Thrills in the Safety Zone," *Chicago Tribune*, July 22, 1988.

55. Thom Shanker, "Soviet War Hero Turns to PR Front," *Chicago Tribune*, July 27, 1989.

56. Cindy Richards, "His Career Is Finding the Right Match," *Chicago Sun Times*, July 3, 1989.

57. Desiree Chen, "Air and Water Show Like D-Day at the Beach," *Chicago Tribune*, July 29, 1991.

58. Steve Dale, "For Soaring Eyes—Navy's Blue Angels Return to Chicago Skies as Part of the Air and Sea Extravaganza," *Chicago Tribune*, July 10, 1992.

59. Ultimate Aircraft Company, http://moleski.net/ULTBIPE/ulthist.htm.

60. Lomcevak, http://www.fightercombat.com/pages/lomcevak.html.

61. *Chicago Tribune*, "Love of Flying Shows in the Announcer's Booth," July 21, 1994.

62. B-2 bomber, http://www.airforce-technology.com/projects/b2.

63. Susan Dodge, "Show Is Pilot's Boyhood Dream," *Chicago Sun Times*, August 24, 1997.

64. Bill Jauss, "Loud, Low-Flying Jets Leave Trachsel Steaming at Ump," *Chicago Tribune*, August 24, 1998.

65. Michael Sneed, "Is the Indiana Toll Road Run by Trolls?" *Chicago Sun Times*, August 25, 1999.

66. William Presecky and Bob Merrifield, "Folks Looking for a Backstage View of this Weekend's Chicago Air and Water Show," *Chicago Tribune*, August 19, 1999.

67. Heather Vogell, "Show's Old Tricks Still Thrill Crowds," *Chicago Tribune*, August 20, 2000.

CHAPTER 7

68. Celeste Busk, "Top Fun: Air and Water Show," *Chicago Sun Times*, August 16, 2002.

ABOUT THE AUTHORS

G erry and Janet Souter have lived in the Chicago area nearly all their lives. Gerry Souter's background includes over thirty years' involvement with aviation; he has flown in balloons, jet fighters and single-engine planes and has written about Canadian bush pilots, Arizona crop-dusters and Gulf of Mexico helicopter fleets.

Janet Souter, president of their company, Avril 1 Group, Inc., edits all of their joint copy and shares Gerry's interest in history. Janet has joined him in balloon, helicopter and light aircraft flights. They are authors of over forty books—histories, biographies and young adult nonfiction. Their most recent book, written for The History Press, is titled *Arlington Heights: A Brief History.*

Top: Gerry Souter with his Nikon on the Chicago Water Department boat off North Avenue Beach—the best seat in the house in 2009. *Courtesy Janet Souter.*

Bottom: Janet Souter in the rear cockpit of an AT-6 Texan prop-driven aerobatic plane before takeoff from the Gary Jet Center. *Courtesy Gerry Souter.*

Visit us at
www.historypress.net